Python API Development With Flask

Mastering Flask: Building Fast, Scalable APIs with Python for the Modern Develope

SIMON TELLIER

 First edition

Published in 2025

TABLE OF CONTENTS

CHAPTER 1: INTRODUCTION TO FLASK AND SETTING UP YOUR ENVIRONMENT

1.1. Overview of Flask: What Makes It Ideal for API Development

Flask is a lightweight, flexible web framework for Python that has quickly gained popularity among developers for building APIs and web applications. Its simplicity, extensibility, and rich ecosystem make it a favorite choice for many developers. Flask is designed with a "micro-framework" philosophy, meaning it comes with the bare essentials to get an application running, but leaves the developer in control of adding any additional features as needed.

This flexibility is what makes Flask such an ideal choice for API development. Unlike more monolithic frameworks, Flask provides a minimalistic foundation that allows you to define and build APIs exactly as you need them. Developers have the freedom to use only the parts of Flask that are necessary for their application, making it efficient and scalable. Whether you're building a small API for a personal project or a large-scale production application, Flask's lightweight nature allows for rapid development and easy maintainability.

One of the key features that makes Flask particularly suitable for API development is its built-in support for routing and request handling. Flask's routing system is simple to use, allowing developers to define endpoints for their APIs easily. The framework also supports HTTP methods like GET, POST, PUT, and DELETE, which are fundamental for building RESTful APIs. This makes Flask a natural fit for REST API development.

Additionally, Flask's ability to integrate seamlessly with various databases, libraries, and tools is another factor that makes it highly adaptable for building APIs. Flask supports popular libraries for database management, like SQLAlchemy, and can be used with NoSQL databases like MongoDB. Flask's modular design allows developers to incorporate libraries for authentication, caching, validation, and more without having to worry about the framework imposing unnecessary restrictions.

In the context of API development, Flask also shines in terms of its developer-friendly environment. Flask applications are easy to set up, and the framework includes a built-in development server, automatic reloading, and debugging tools that make it easy for developers to test and refine their APIs. The straightforwardness of the framework allows new developers to get up and running quickly, while its flexibility ensures that more experienced developers can implement complex features with ease.

In essence, Flask is a framework that provides the building blocks for creating web applications and APIs, but leaves enough freedom for developers to structure their projects in a way that suits their specific needs. It provides an efficient, clean, and easily maintainable solution for developers looking to build scalable, high-performance APIs.

1.2. History and Evolution of Flask

Flask was created by Armin Ronacher in 2010, as part of a project to provide a minimalistic and easy-to-use Python web framework that would allow developers to build web applications quickly. The project started as a simple experiment with no real intention of evolving into a large framework. Ronacher, who had previously worked with the Werkzeug library (a collection of WSGI utilities for Python), wanted to create something that would offer more control and customization for developers compared to the heavy, full-stack web frameworks available at the time.

The first version of Flask was designed to be small, modular, and lightweight, with the core focus being simplicity and flexibility. Rather than imposing a rigid structure, Flask would allow developers to use the tools and libraries they preferred, enabling them to easily create APIs and web applications. The framework was built on top of two key components: **Werkzeug** (a WSGI utility library) and **Jinja2** (a templating engine). These components provided the foundation for Flask’s routing and templating capabilities.

Flask’s early popularity stemmed from its ease of use and developer-friendly design. It quickly garnered attention from developers who found it easier to work with than the more complex and opinionated frameworks like Django. Flask’s simplicity made it appealing to both newcomers to web development and experienced developers who wanted a lightweight framework with fewer abstractions.

As Flask's popularity grew, its ecosystem began to expand, with third-party extensions for adding database support, authentication, form handling, and more. These extensions allowed Flask to maintain its lightweight, modular nature while still providing powerful features that developers could incorporate as needed. Flask’s community also grew rapidly, with a wealth of documentation, tutorials, and community-contributed extensions becoming available online.

One of the most significant changes in Flask’s evolution was its adoption in the microservices architecture movement. Developers began to embrace Flask’s simplicity and flexibility in building microservices-based applications. Flask’s ability to handle API requests and scale independently made it an ideal candidate for this new architectural paradigm.

In recent years, Flask has continued to evolve with regular updates, improvements, and a focus on maintaining compatibility with Python 3. Flask’s core developers have continued to release bug fixes, performance improvements, and new features, ensuring the framework remains relevant in an ever-changing software development landscape.

Today, Flask is widely used in both small-scale and enterprise-level applications. Its simple yet powerful design continues to make it a go-to choice for developers building APIs and web applications. The flexibility of Flask means it can be used for a wide range of projects, from single-page apps to complex enterprise solutions.

1.3. Flask vs. Other Web Frameworks (Django, FastAPI, etc.)

While Flask has grown to become one of the most popular frameworks for Python web development, it is not the only option available. Other frameworks, such as Django and FastAPI, offer different approaches to web development, and each has its strengths and weaknesses. In this section, we will compare Flask with two of its most notable competitors: **Django** and **FastAPI**.

Flask vs. Django

Django is another widely used Python web framework, but it takes a different approach compared to Flask. While Flask is considered a micro-framework, Django is a full-stack framework that provides a more opinionated structure and comes with many built-in features. Django's "batteries-included" philosophy means it includes everything you need to build a web application, including an ORM, authentication system, admin interface, and more.

For developers who want a comprehensive, feature-rich framework out of the box, Django is a solid choice. It is particularly well-suited for developers building large-scale applications that require a lot of built-in functionality. Django enforces a more structured approach to development, which can be helpful for maintaining consistency across larger teams and projects. The framework also comes with a robust set of security features, which makes it a good choice for building secure web applications.

However, Flask's minimalism sets it apart from Django. Flask provides more flexibility and allows developers to choose their libraries and tools, making it an ideal choice for those who need more control over their project structure. While Django is excellent for rapid development of complex web applications, Flask is better suited for developers who prefer a more lightweight, customizable approach.

Flask vs. FastAPI

FastAPI is a newer Python web framework that has gained popularity for its speed and ease of use, particularly when building APIs. Like Flask, FastAPI is designed with performance in mind, but it offers several key features that make it unique. FastAPI is built on top of Python's type hints and uses asynchronous programming by default, making it particularly well-suited for handling high-performance APIs and real-time applications.

One of the standout features of FastAPI is its automatic generation of OpenAPI and JSON Schema documentation. FastAPI can generate interactive API documentation automatically based on the endpoints defined in the application, which is a significant advantage for API development. Flask, on the other hand, does not provide this feature out of the box and requires additional libraries or manual integration to generate API documentation.

FastAPI also leverages asynchronous programming with **asyncio**, making it highly efficient for handling a large number of simultaneous connections. This makes FastAPI an excellent choice for applications that require real-time communication, such as chat applications or live data feeds.

However, while FastAPI's speed and features make it an excellent choice for building modern APIs, Flask's simplicity and wide adoption make it a go-to framework for many developers. Flask's extensive ecosystem, rich documentation, and broad community support are hard to match, especially for developers who are looking for a straightforward, well-documented solution for building APIs.

The choice between Flask, Django, and FastAPI comes down to the needs of the project. Flask is perfect for developers who need flexibility and control over their application structure. Django is ideal for large, feature-rich applications that need an all-in-one framework. FastAPI is a great option for building high-performance APIs and applications that rely on asynchronous operations. Each framework has its strengths, and the right choice depends on the specific requirements of the project at hand.

1.4. Setting Up Python and Flask

Before diving into Flask development, it's important to get your environment set up properly. This will ensure that you have the necessary tools installed and that your project is structured in a way that's easy to maintain. Setting up Python and Flask is a relatively simple process that you can complete in a few steps.

Step 1: Install Python

Flask is a Python framework, so the first thing you need to do is ensure you have Python installed on your system. Flask is compatible with Python 3, so it's recommended to use a version of Python 3. You can download Python from the official Python website at https://www.python.org/downloads/. The website will detect your operating system and suggest the appropriate version for you.

Once Python is installed, verify the installation by opening your terminal (or command prompt on Windows) and typing:

bash

Copy

```
python --version
```

This should return something like Python 3.x.x, indicating that Python is successfully installed.

Step 2: Install pip

pip is the package installer for Python, and it is used to install libraries and dependencies like Flask. If you've installed Python 3.4 or later, pip is already included by default. You can check if pip is installed by running:

bash

Copy

```
pip --version
```

If you see a version number, pip is installed. If not, you can install pip by following the instructions from the official documentation.

Step 3: Install Flask

With Python and pip installed, you're ready to install Flask. Open your terminal or command prompt and run the following command:

bash

Copy

```
pip install Flask
```

This will download and install Flask and all of its dependencies. Flask is a lightweight framework, so it doesn't have many dependencies, which makes the installation process quick and straightforward.

After installation, you can verify that Flask has been installed by running:

bash

Copy

```
python -m flask --version
```

This should return the Flask version, confirming that Flask is ready to use.

1.5. Creating Your First Flask Project

Now that your environment is set up and Flask is installed, it's time to create your first Flask project. This will involve writing some simple Python code to create a basic Flask web application, setting up routes, and running the application on your local server.

Step 1: Create a Project Folder

First, create a folder on your computer where you'll store your Flask project. You can name it anything, but for this example, let's call it flask_project. Inside this folder, you will create the necessary Python files and folders for your project.

bash

Copy

```
mkdir flask_project
cd flask_project
```

Step 2: Create a Python Script for Your Flask App

Inside the flask_project folder, create a new Python file called app.py. This file will contain the code for your Flask application. Open this file in your preferred text editor (like VS Code, Sublime Text, or PyCharm), and add the following code:

python

Copy

```
from flask import Flask

app = Flask(__name__)

@app.route('/')
def hello_world():
    return 'Hello, World!'

if __name__ == '__main__':
    app.run(debug=True)
```

Here's what's happening in the code:

- We import the Flask class from the flask module.
- We create an instance of the Flask class, which will represent our application.
- We define a route using the @app.route() decorator. This route tells Flask to respond to HTTP requests made to the root URL (/), and the function hello_world() will return the message Hello, World!.
- Finally, we run the Flask application with app.run(debug=True). The debug=True option allows for live reloading and better error messages during development.

Step 3: Run Your Flask Application

To run your Flask application, navigate to the flask_project folder in your terminal, and run the following command:

bash

Copy

```
python app.py
```

If everything is set up correctly, you'll see output in your terminal that looks like this:

csharp

Copy

```
* Running on http://127.0.0.1:5000/ (Press CTRL+C to quit)
```

This means your Flask application is now running on your local machine at the specified URL (http://127.0.0.1:5000/). Open a web browser and go to that address, and you should see the message "Hello, World!" displayed.

1.6. Using Virtual Environments for Clean Development

When developing any Python application, it's best practice to use a **virtual environment**. A virtual environment isolates your project's dependencies from the global Python environment, ensuring that each project has its own set of dependencies that won't conflict with other projects. This is particularly useful when you're working with multiple Flask projects, each potentially requiring different versions of libraries.

Step 1: Install `virtualenv`

The first step is to install the `virtualenv` package, which helps you create isolated Python environments. You can install it globally using pip:

bash

Copy

```
pip install virtualenv
```

Step 2: Create a Virtual Environment

Next, navigate to your flask_project folder and create a virtual environment. Run the following command:

bash

Copy

```
python -m venv venv
```

This will create a new directory called venv inside your project folder, which will contain the isolated Python environment.

Step 3: Activate the Virtual Environment

Before you start installing any dependencies, you need to activate the virtual environment. The process differs depending on your operating system.

On Windows, run:

bash

Copy

```
.\venv\Scripts\activate
```

- **On macOS/Linux**, run:

  bash

  Copy

  ```
  source venv/bin/activate
  ```

When the virtual environment is activated, you should see (venv) at the beginning of your terminal prompt, indicating that any Python packages you install will be confined to the virtual environment.

Step 4: Install Flask Inside the Virtual Environment

With your virtual environment activated, you can now install Flask:

bash

Copy

```
pip install Flask
```

This will install Flask only in the virtual environment, not globally. You can also install any other libraries your project might need, and they'll be confined to this environment.

Step 5: Deactivate the Virtual Environment

When you're finished working on your project, you can deactivate the virtual environment by running:

bash

Copy

```
deactivate
```

This will return you to the global Python environment. When you want to work on the project again, you can activate the virtual environment using the same command as before.

Using virtual environments is an important practice in Python development because it ensures that each project can have its own dependencies without affecting other projects. This helps you avoid dependency conflicts and ensures that your application will run smoothly across different machines.

In this chapter, we've walked through the basic steps of setting up Python and Flask on your system, creating your first Flask application, and using virtual environments for clean development. These foundational steps will allow you to begin building powerful APIs and web applications with Flask. Now that your environment is set up and you've seen how to create a simple Flask app, you're ready to move on to more complex projects and dive deeper into Flask's powerful features.

Chapter 2: Basic Flask API Architecture

2.1. Introduction to RESTful APIs

When developing APIs with Flask, it's essential to understand the core principles behind RESTful APIs. REST (Representational State Transfer) is an architectural style that defines a set of rules and constraints for building web services. It leverages the power of HTTP and aims to make APIs scalable, stateless, and easily maintainable.

What is REST?

At its core, REST is a set of guidelines that dictate how data should be structured and transmitted over the web. RESTful APIs are designed around the idea of **resources**, which are entities that the API interacts with. Resources can be anything—users, products, posts, or even more abstract concepts like transactions or logs. Each resource is uniquely identified by a URL (Uniform Resource Locator), and the API exposes endpoints (URLs) through which clients can interact with these resources.

The guiding principles of REST focus on the following key aspects:

- **Statelessness:** Each request from a client to a server must contain all the necessary information to process the request. The server should not store any information about the client between requests. Each request is independent, making the system more scalable and resilient.
- **Client-Server Architecture:** REST APIs follow a clear separation between the client (which makes requests) and the server (which processes the requests). This allows for easier development and scaling, as the client and server can evolve independently.

- **Uniform Interface:** REST APIs provide a standard way of interacting with resources, usually through HTTP methods and URLs. This uniformity allows clients to interact with different APIs in a consistent way.
- **Representation:** Resources are represented in a format that can be easily understood and processed, typically using formats like JSON or XML. When a client interacts with a resource, it receives the resource's representation (such as a JSON object) in response.

A RESTful API typically exposes a set of **endpoints** (URLs) that allow clients to perform operations on resources. These operations correspond to standard HTTP methods like GET, POST, PUT, and DELETE, which will be discussed in more detail later.

Why Use REST?

RESTful APIs are widely used because they follow a simple, predictable pattern that is easy to implement, understand, and maintain. They are lightweight and use standard HTTP methods, making them ideal for web and mobile applications. Since REST relies on standard HTTP protocols, it is compatible with most web browsers, mobile platforms, and other services, making it a flexible choice for developers.

For Flask, implementing RESTful APIs is incredibly straightforward due to Flask's simplicity and ease of use. Flask's routing system allows you to define routes for each of your resources and implement the logic for handling requests made to those routes.

2.2. Understanding HTTP Methods (GET, POST, PUT, DELETE)

When working with RESTful APIs, understanding the four primary HTTP methods—GET, POST, PUT, and DELETE—is crucial. These methods define how clients interact with the resources exposed by the API.

GET Method

The **GET** method is used to retrieve data from the server. When a client sends a GET request to a specific endpoint, it is asking the server to return the current state or representation of the resource. GET requests are **idempotent**, meaning that multiple identical GET requests will have the same result and won't cause any side effects on the resource.

Example:

http
Copy
```
GET /api/users
```

This request would retrieve a list of users from the server. In Flask, you would typically use the `@app.route()` decorator to define a route for handling GET requests.

Flask Example:

python
Copy
```
@app.route('/api/users', methods=['GET'])
def get_users():
    return jsonify(users)
```

Here, the `get_users` function handles GET requests to the `/api/users` route and returns a JSON representation of the `users` data.

POST Method

The **POST** method is used to send data to the server, usually to create a new resource. When a client sends a POST request, it typically includes a payload (often in JSON format) that contains the data for the new resource. Unlike GET, POST is **non-idempotent**, meaning that sending the same POST request multiple times may create multiple resources.

Example:

http

Copy

```
POST /api/users
```

This request would create a new user on the server. The client would send data (such as a name and email) in the request body, and the server would create a new user based on that data.

Flask Example:

python

Copy

```
@app.route('/api/users', methods=['POST'])
def create_user():
    data = request.get_json()
    new_user = User(name=data['name'], email=data['email'])
    db.session.add(new_user)
    db.session.commit()
    return jsonify(new_user), 201
```

In this example, the create_user function receives the data sent in the POST request, creates a new user, and stores it in the database.

PUT Method

The **PUT** method is used to update an existing resource on the server. It requires the client to send the updated data in the request body. Unlike POST, PUT is **idempotent**, meaning that sending the same PUT request multiple times will always result in the same resource state.

Example:

http

Copy

```
PUT /api/users/123
```

This request would update the user with ID 123 on the server. The client would send the new data for that user, and the server would update the resource accordingly.

Flask Example:

python

Copy

```
@app.route('/api/users/<int:id>', methods=['PUT'])
def update_user(id):
    data = request.get_json()
    user = User.query.get(id)
    if user:
        user.name = data['name']
        user.email = data['email']
        db.session.commit()
```

```
        return jsonify(user)
    return jsonify({'error': 'User not found'}), 404
```

In this example, the update_user function updates the details of the user identified by id. It first retrieves the user from the database, applies the changes, and then commits the update.

DELETE Method

The **DELETE** method is used to delete a resource on the server. When a client sends a DELETE request, it is asking the server to remove the specified resource. Like GET, DELETE requests are **idempotent**, meaning that sending the same DELETE request multiple times will have the same result (the resource is deleted).

Example:

http

Copy

```
DELETE /api/users/123
```

This request would delete the user with ID 123 from the server.

Flask Example:

python

Copy

```
@app.route('/api/users/<int:id>', methods=['DELETE'])
def delete_user(id):
    user = User.query.get(id)
    if user:
        db.session.delete(user)
```

```
        db.session.commit()
        return jsonify({'message': 'User deleted'})
    return jsonify({'error': 'User not found'}), 404
```

In this example, the delete_user function deletes the user identified by id. It first checks if the user exists in the database, deletes the user if found, and then returns a confirmation message.

2.3. Flask Core Concepts: Routes, Requests, and Responses

At the heart of any Flask application are the **routes**, **requests**, and **responses**. These are the core concepts that define how Flask handles HTTP interactions between the client and server.

Routes

In Flask, routes define the URLs that a client can request. Each route is associated with a specific function that processes the request and generates a response. Routes are defined using the @app.route() decorator, which binds a function to a specific URL and HTTP method.

For example, to create a route for handling requests to the /api/users endpoint, you can define a function like this:

python

Copy

```
@app.route('/api/users', methods=['GET'])
def get_users():
    return jsonify(users)
```

Here, the route /api/users is associated with the get_users function, which is called whenever a GET request is made to that URL. Flask's routing system also allows for dynamic URLs, where parts of the URL can be passed as arguments to the route handler:

python
Copy
```
@app.route('/api/users/<int:id>', methods=['GET'])
def get_user(id):
    user = User.query.get(id)
    return jsonify(user)
```

In this example, <int:id> specifies that the id portion of the URL should be passed to the get_user function as an argument.

Requests

A **request** is the data that the client sends to the server. It includes information such as the HTTP method (GET, POST, PUT, DELETE), any URL parameters, headers, and the body of the request (if applicable).

Flask provides the request object, which allows you to access the data in the incoming request. You can use request.args to get query parameters, request.form to get form data, and request.get_json() to access JSON data sent in a POST or PUT request.

Example of handling a POST request with JSON data:

python
Copy
```
from flask import request
```

```
@app.route('/api/users', methods=['POST'])
def create_user():
    data = request.get_json()
    # Handle the request and create the user
```

Responses

A **response** is the data that the server sends back to the client. Flask provides the `response` object, which you can use to return the desired output from your route handler.

Flask also allows you to return a variety of response types, including simple strings, HTML templates, or JSON data. When building APIs, you'll often use `jsonify()` to return JSON responses, as shown in the examples above.

You can also set response headers and status codes using Flask's `make_response()` function:

python

Copy

```
from flask import make_response, jsonify

@app.route('/api/users')
def get_users():
    response = make_response(jsonify(users), 200)
    response.headers['X-Custom-Header'] = 'Custom value'
    return response
```

In this example, we create a custom response, set the status code to 200 (OK), and add a custom header to the response.

With these fundamental concepts in place—RESTful APIs, HTTP methods, and Flask's routing system—you're now equipped to start building APIs with Flask. Next, we'll dive deeper into working with databases and performing CRUD operations to bring your API to life.

2.4. Building Your First API: A Simple GET Endpoint

Now that we've covered the foundational concepts of RESTful APIs, HTTP methods, and Flask core components, it's time to create your first API. This will be a simple API with a single **GET** endpoint, which is one of the most common operations you'll encounter when building RESTful APIs.

Setting Up Your Project Structure

Start by creating a folder for your project, like we did in the previous chapter. Let's call it simple_flask_api. Inside the folder, create a new file called app.py. This file will contain the main Flask application logic.

To begin, let's create a simple GET endpoint that returns a list of users. We will simulate user data using a Python list.

1. **Create a Python file (app.py)** and start by importing Flask:

python

Copy

```
from flask import Flask, jsonify

app = Flask(__name__)

@app.route('/api/users', methods=['GET'])
```

```
def get_users():
    # Sample user data
    users = [
        {'id': 1, 'name': 'Alice', 'email': 'alice@example.com'},
        {'id': 2, 'name': 'Bob', 'email': 'bob@example.com'},
        {'id': 3, 'name': 'Charlie', 'email': 'charlie@example.com'}
    ]
    return jsonify(users)

if __name__ == '__main__':
    app.run(debug=True)
```

Breakdown of the Code:

- We begin by importing the necessary modules, specifically Flask and jsonify. jsonify is a Flask utility that turns Python objects into JSON responses, which is ideal for APIs.
- Flask(__name__) initializes the Flask application. The __name__ argument is used to define the app's context.
- The @app.route('/api/users', methods=['GET']) decorator defines a route. This route handles GET requests at the URL /api/users.
- The get_users function simulates fetching data from a database by using a Python list containing user dictionaries. Each user has an id, name, and email attribute.
- The jsonify() function takes the users list and converts it into a JSON response.
- Finally, app.run(debug=True) starts the Flask development server with debugging enabled, so the app will automatically reload when changes are made.

Running Your API

To run your API, navigate to the project directory in your terminal and type:

bash

Copy

```
python app.py
```

Your Flask app will start running locally on http://127.0.0.1:5000/. Open your browser and visit:

arduino

Copy

```
http://127.0.0.1:5000/api/users
```

You should see a JSON response with the list of users:

json

Copy

```
[
  {"id": 1, "name": "Alice", "email": "alice@example.com"},
  {"id": 2, "name": "Bob", "email": "bob@example.com"},
  {"id": 3, "name": "Charlie", "email": "charlie@example.com"}
]
```

What's Happening Under the Hood?

When a client sends a **GET** request to /api/users, Flask calls the get_users function. Inside this function, we define a list of users and return it as a JSON response using the jsonify() function. Flask automatically serializes the Python list into JSON format, and sets the appropriate HTTP headers (such as Content-Type: application/json).

This simple API demonstrates how easy it is to expose data using Flask and handle HTTP GET requests.

2.5. Flask Blueprints: Structuring Large Applications

As your application grows, you'll likely encounter the need to break it down into smaller, more manageable components. This is where **Flask Blueprints** come into play. Blueprints allow you to organize your application by grouping related routes and logic into distinct modules. This makes your code easier to maintain and scale as your project evolves.

What Are Blueprints?

A **Blueprint** in Flask is essentially a way to organize a set of routes and their handlers into a reusable module. By using blueprints, you can keep your application modular and ensure that related functionality is kept together in separate files. This approach is particularly helpful for large projects where different components (such as users, products, or orders) need their own set of routes.

Setting Up Blueprints

Let's break your simple API from earlier into two parts: one for handling user-related functionality and another for handling other features (if you had them). Here's how you can structure your project using blueprints:

1. **Create a new directory for the project structure:**

bash

Copy

```
simple_flask_api/
├── app.py
├── users/
│   ├── __init__.py
│   ├── routes.py
└── __init__.py
```

- The users/routes.py file will contain all user-related endpoints.
- The app.py file will import and register the blueprint for handling the users.

2. **Define the Blueprint in users/routes.py:**

python

Copy

```python
from flask import Blueprint, jsonify

users_blueprint = Blueprint('users', __name__)

@users_blueprint.route('/api/users', methods=['GET'])
def get_users():
    users = [
        {'id': 1, 'name': 'Alice', 'email': 'alice@example.com'},
        {'id': 2, 'name': 'Bob', 'email': 'bob@example.com'},
        {'id': 3, 'name': 'Charlie', 'email': 'charlie@example.com'}
    ]
    return jsonify(users)
```

Here, we define a users_blueprint object using the Blueprint class. This blueprint will contain the route for the /api/users endpoint.

3. **Register the Blueprint in app.py:**

Now, in the main app.py file, we need to import and register the blueprint:

python

Copy

```
from flask import Flask
from users.routes import users_blueprint

app = Flask(__name__)
app.register_blueprint(users_blueprint)

if __name__ == '__main__':
    app.run(debug=True)
```

In this file, we import the users_blueprint and register it with the Flask application instance using app.register_blueprint(). This tells Flask to include all the routes defined in users.routes as part of the application.

Benefits of Using Blueprints

- **Modularization:** Blueprints help you separate different concerns in your application. For example, all routes related to users can live in the users blueprint, while routes for products can be in a products blueprint, and so on.

- **Reusability:** Blueprints make it easier to reuse code across different applications or environments. You can package a blueprint into a separate module or package, making it reusable in other projects.
- **Collaboration:** In large teams, blueprints allow developers to work on different sections of the application independently. One developer can work on the users blueprint while another works on the products blueprint without interfering with each other's code.

2.6. Organizing Project Files for Scalability and Maintainability

As your Flask application grows, you'll want to adopt an organized folder structure that is scalable and easy to maintain. Structuring your project correctly from the start will save you time and headaches later on.

Recommended Project Structure

Here's an example of a project structure that is suitable for larger Flask applications:

arduino

Copy

```
simple_flask_api/
  ├── app/
  │   ├── __init__.py
  │   ├── routes.py
  │   ├── models.py
  │   ├── config.py
  ├── users/
  │   ├── __init__.py
  │   ├── routes.py
```

```
│   ├── models.py
├── requirements.txt
├── app.py
├── config.py
└── run.py
```

Breakdown of the Structure

- **app/**: This directory contains the main application logic. It includes files for routes, models, and configuration settings.
    - __init__.py: Initializes the Flask app and imports the necessary modules.
    - routes.py: Contains the routes for the application.
    - models.py: Defines the database models for the app (if you're using a database).
    - config.py: Holds configuration settings such as the environment (development or production), database URI, and other settings.
- **users/**: This directory contains all user-related logic, such as user models, routes, and handlers. You can create separate directories for each resource in your app (e.g., products/, orders/, etc.).
- **requirements.txt**: Lists the dependencies for the project. You can create this file by running:

bash

Copy

```
pip freeze > requirements.txt
```

- **app.py**: This is the entry point for the application, where you initialize the app and register blueprints.

- run.py: A script to run the application. It's often used to provide configuration settings or to handle special requirements before starting the app.

Benefits of This Structure

- **Scalability**: As your application grows, this structure allows you to add more resources (e.g., products, orders) by creating additional directories similar to users/.
- **Separation of Concerns**: By organizing the application into separate modules, each focusing on a specific task (routes, models, etc.), your code remains clean and easy to manage.
- **Easier Collaboration**: This structure makes it easy for multiple developers to work on the same project simultaneously, each focusing on a specific area of functionality.

In this chapter, we've built upon the basic concepts of Flask to create a simple API with a GET endpoint. We explored how to organize Flask applications using blueprints, which help maintain modularity, reusability, and scalability. Lastly, we discussed the importance of structuring your project files to ensure maintainability as your application grows. With this solid foundation, you can now build more complex APIs with Flask, knowing that you have a structure that supports both scalability and clean development practices.

Chapter 3: Building Your First API

3.1. Designing API Endpoints

Designing effective API endpoints is a crucial step in building a well-organized and easy-to-use RESTful API. The endpoint is the URL where a client can send requests to interact with a specific resource or collection of resources. When designing your API endpoints, you should consider factors like readability, consistency, and whether the endpoint reflects the action it performs.

RESTful Design Principles

In RESTful APIs, endpoints should be designed around **resources**, which are the entities that clients interact with. Resources could be anything: users, products, posts, or even abstract concepts like transactions or settings. Each resource should have its own unique URL, and the actions (like retrieving, creating, updating, or deleting) should be expressed via HTTP methods (GET, POST, PUT, DELETE).

1. **Resource URLs (Nouns):** The endpoint should reflect the name of the resource it represents. The resource name should be plural to represent collections of resources. For example, the URL for accessing a collection of users could be `/api/users`, while the URL for accessing a single user could be `/api/users/1`, where `1` is the ID of the user.
   Examples:
   - `GET /api/users` — Retrieves all users.
   - `GET /api/users/1` — Retrieves the user with ID 1.
   - `POST /api/users` — Creates a new user.
   - `PUT /api/users/1` — Updates the user with ID 1.
   - `DELETE /api/users/1` — Deletes the user with ID 1.

2. **Use of HTTP Methods:** HTTP methods (GET, POST, PUT, DELETE) describe the action that is performed on the resource. It's important to keep your endpoints aligned with these HTTP methods to ensure that the API follows REST principles.
   - **GET**: Retrieves information about a resource or a collection.
   - **POST**: Creates a new resource.
   - **PUT**: Updates an existing resource.
   - **DELETE**: Deletes a resource.

Best Practices for Designing Endpoints

- **Consistency**: Keep the naming conventions consistent across your API. For example, use `/users` for the user collection and `/users/{id}` for a specific user.
- **Use Plural Nouns**: Always use plural nouns for resource names to maintain consistency when accessing multiple entities.
- **Avoid Nested Routes**: Try to avoid unnecessary nesting in your routes. A route like `/users/1/posts` to get posts for a specific user is fine, but `/users/1/posts/2/comments` might become overly complex. Instead, consider flattening the hierarchy.
- **RESTful Standards**: Stick to REST conventions. If you need to provide a relationship between two resources (e.g., a user and their posts), use `GET /users/{user_id}/posts` to get a user's posts.

3.2. Handling JSON Data with Flask

In most modern APIs, **JSON** (JavaScript Object Notation) is the preferred data format for sending and receiving data. Flask provides easy-to-use tools for handling JSON, allowing you to seamlessly parse and send JSON data in your API.

Sending JSON Responses

Flask provides the jsonify() function to convert Python dictionaries, lists, or other serializable objects into JSON format. This is essential when returning data from your API endpoints, as clients expect to receive data in a standard format like JSON.

Example of sending a JSON response:

python

Copy

```
from flask import Flask, jsonify

app = Flask(__name__)

@app.route('/api/users', methods=['GET'])
def get_users():
    users = [
        {'id': 1, 'name': 'Alice', 'email': 'alice@example.com'},
        {'id': 2, 'name': 'Bob', 'email': 'bob@example.com'},
    ]
    return jsonify(users)

if __name__ == '__main__':
    app.run(debug=True)
```

In this example, the get_users function sends a list of user dictionaries, and jsonify(users) converts it into JSON format. Flask automatically sets the Content-Type header to application/json, indicating that the response is in JSON format.

Receiving JSON Requests

When receiving data from clients, Flask provides the request object, which allows you to easily access data sent in a JSON format. To access JSON data sent in the body of a POST or PUT request, use request.get_json().

Example of receiving JSON data in a POST request:

python

Copy

```
from flask import Flask, request, jsonify


app = Flask(__name__)


@app.route('/api/users', methods=['POST'])
def create_user():
    data = request.get_json()  # Retrieve JSON data from the request body
    name = data['name']
    email = data['email']

    # Simulating saving data to the database
    new_user = {'id': 3, 'name': name, 'email': email}

    return jsonify(new_user), 201  # Return the created user and status code 201


if __name__ == '__main__':
    app.run(debug=True)
```

Here, we use request.get_json() to retrieve the incoming JSON data in the request body. The client is expected to send a JSON object with name and email fields. We then simulate saving the user to a database and return the newly created user as a JSON response.

Handling Errors with JSON

When working with JSON in Flask, it's a good practice to handle potential errors, such as when the client sends malformed JSON or missing fields. You can catch errors and send appropriate responses using Flask's abort function or custom error messages.

Example of handling errors:

python
Copy
```
from flask import Flask, request, jsonify, abort


@app.route('/api/users', methods=['POST'])
def create_user():
    if not request.json or not 'name' in request.json:
        abort(400, description="Bad Request: Missing 'name' field")


    name = request.json['name']
    email = request.json['email'] if 'email' in request.json else None
    new_user = {'id': 3, 'name': name, 'email': email}


    return jsonify(new_user), 201
```

In this example, we check if the incoming request is JSON and if the name field is provided. If not, we return a 400 Bad Request error with a descriptive message.

3.3. Implementing POST, PUT, and DELETE Requests

In addition to the GET method, the POST, PUT, and DELETE HTTP methods are essential for building a fully functioning RESTful API. These methods allow you to create, update, and delete resources in your application. Let's dive into implementing each of these methods using Flask.

Implementing a POST Request

The **POST** method is used to create new resources on the server. When a client sends a POST request, they typically include data in the request body, which the server uses to create a new resource.

In Flask, you can implement a POST request by reading the data from the request, processing it, and returning a response with the created resource.

Example of creating a new user with POST:

python

Copy

```
from flask import Flask, request, jsonify

app = Flask(__name__)

users = []

@app.route('/api/users', methods=['POST'])
def create_user():
```

```
    data = request.get_json()
    name = data['name']
    email = data['email']

    # Simulate creating a new user
    new_user = {'id': len(users) + 1, 'name': name, 'email': email}
    users.append(new_user)

    return jsonify(new_user), 201  # Return the new user and a 201 status code

if __name__ == '__main__':
    app.run(debug=True)
```

In this example, we receive the user's data in JSON format, create a new user object, and append it to a list. The server responds with the newly created user and a 201 Created status code.

Implementing a PUT Request

The **PUT** method is used to update an existing resource. Unlike POST, which creates a new resource, PUT modifies an existing resource. When implementing a PUT request, the client sends data to update a specific resource, and the server processes the update.

Example of updating an existing user with PUT:

python
Copy
```
@app.route('/api/users/<int:id>', methods=['PUT'])
def update_user(id):
    data = request.get_json()
```

```
    user = next((user for user in users if user['id'] == id), None)

    if not user:
        return jsonify({'error': 'User not found'}), 404

    user['name'] = data['name']
    user['email'] = data['email']

    return jsonify(user)
```

In this example, the update_user function searches for the user by their ID and updates their name and email based on the incoming request data. If the user is not found, it returns a 404 Not Found error.

Implementing a DELETE Request

The **DELETE** method is used to delete an existing resource. When a client sends a DELETE request, the server deletes the specified resource.

Example of deleting a user with DELETE:

python
Copy
```
@app.route('/api/users/<int:id>', methods=['DELETE'])
def delete_user(id):
    user = next((user for user in users if user['id'] == id), None)

    if not user:
        return jsonify({'error': 'User not found'}), 404
```

```
users.remove(user)

return jsonify({'message': 'User deleted successfully'}), 200
```

In this example, the `delete_user` function searches for the user by their ID, removes the user from the list if found, and returns a success message.

We covered how to design API endpoints effectively, how to handle JSON data in Flask, and how to implement POST, PUT, and DELETE requests to manage resources. By mastering these core operations, you can now build fully functional, interactive RESTful APIs with Flask. As you progress, you'll be able to create more complex APIs and implement additional functionality such as authentication, pagination, and filtering.

3.4. Response Codes and Status Messages

In any RESTful API, response codes (also known as HTTP status codes) are an essential component for conveying the outcome of a request. They provide useful information about whether the request was successful or if there was an issue that needs to be addressed. In Flask, you can return custom status codes and status messages, allowing you to communicate the result of an API operation clearly and consistently.

Understanding HTTP Status Codes

HTTP status codes are grouped into five categories:

1. **1xx (Informational)** – These are provisional responses. They're rarely used in practice.
    - Example: `100 Continue`

2. **2xx (Success)** – Indicates that the request was successfully received, understood, and processed by the server.
    - Example: 200 OK, 201 Created
3. **3xx (Redirection)** – Indicates that further action is required to complete the request. Often used when resources have been moved.
    - Example: 301 Moved Permanently
4. **4xx (Client Errors)** – The client seems to have made a mistake in the request.
    - Example: 400 Bad Request, 404 Not Found, 401 Unauthorized
5. **5xx (Server Errors)** – The server encountered an error or is otherwise incapable of performing the request.
    - Example: 500 Internal Server Error, 502 Bad Gateway

Common Status Codes for API Responses

When building an API, you'll need to use specific HTTP status codes to indicate whether the request was successful or if an error occurred. Here are some of the most commonly used status codes:

- **200 OK**: The request was successful, and the server has returned the requested data.
    - Example: Returning data from a GET request.
- **201 Created**: The request was successful, and a new resource was created.
    - Example: Successfully creating a new user via a POST request.
- **204 No Content**: The request was successful, but there is no content to return.
    - Example: Successfully deleting a resource via a DELETE request.
- **400 Bad Request**: The request was malformed or missing required parameters.
    - Example: A POST request without the required fields (e.g., missing name or email for a user).
- **404 Not Found**: The requested resource could not be found on the server.
    - Example: Trying to access a user that doesn't exist via a GET request.

- **500 Internal Server Error**: The server encountered an unexpected condition.
    - Example: A database failure or server crash.

Sending Custom Status Codes in Flask

In Flask, you can customize the response status codes by using the response object or returning a tuple with the response data and status code.

Example of using status codes in Flask:

python

Copy

```
from flask import Flask, jsonify

app = Flask(__name__)

@app.route('/api/users', methods=['GET'])
def get_users():
    users = [{'id': 1, 'name': 'Alice'}, {'id': 2, 'name': 'Bob'}]

    if not users:
        return jsonify({'message': 'No users found'}), 404  # 404 Not Found

    return jsonify(users), 200  # 200 OK

if __name__ == '__main__':
    app.run(debug=True)
```

In this example, if the list of users is empty, we return a 404 Not Found status with a message indicating that no users were found. If users exist, we return them with a 200 OK status code.

3.5. Error Handling: Flask's Built-in Error Handling

Error handling is a critical aspect of building robust APIs. Flask provides built-in mechanisms for handling errors gracefully, ensuring that clients receive meaningful error messages when something goes wrong. Effective error handling helps improve the developer experience by providing clear explanations of what went wrong and what needs to be done to resolve the issue.

Handling Client Errors with abort()

Flask provides the abort() function to immediately stop processing a request and return an HTTP error code. This is useful when the request doesn't meet the necessary conditions.

For example, if a client tries to update a user but doesn't provide a name, you might want to abort the request and return a 400 Bad Request error.

Example of using abort() to handle client errors:

python
Copy

```
from flask import Flask, request, jsonify, abort

app = Flask(__name__)

@app.route('/api/users', methods=['POST'])
```

```
def create_user():
    if not request.json or 'name' not in request.json:
        abort(400, description="Bad Request: Missing 'name' field")

    name = request.json['name']
    new_user = {'id': 1, 'name': name}

    return jsonify(new_user), 201

if __name__ == '__main__':
    app.run(debug=True)
```

In this example, if the request doesn't contain JSON or the name field is missing, we call abort(400) to send a 400 Bad Request error, with a custom error message.

Handling Server Errors and Custom Error Pages

While client errors are often handled using abort(), server errors (like database issues) can be handled by Flask's built-in error handlers. Flask allows you to define custom error handlers for specific HTTP error codes, such as 404 Not Found or 500 Internal Server Error.

Example of handling server errors:

python

Copy

```
@app.errorhandler(404)
def not_found_error(error):
    return jsonify({'message': 'Resource not found'}), 404
```

```
@app.errorhandler(500)
def internal_server_error(error):
    return jsonify({'message': 'Internal server error, please try again later'}), 500
```

In this example:

- When a 404 error occurs (e.g., when a route doesn't exist), Flask will call the not_found_error function and return a custom message and status code.
- If a 500 error occurs (e.g., a database failure), Flask will call the internal_server_error function and return a message indicating a server error.

You can also create custom error handlers for other HTTP status codes, making your API more user-friendly and less prone to generic error messages.

3.6. Testing Your API Locally

Testing is a crucial step in ensuring that your API works as expected. Flask provides several tools to make testing your application easy and straightforward, even during the development process. The goal is to verify that each endpoint is functioning correctly, handling errors as expected, and responding with the correct status codes.

Testing with Flask's Built-in Test Client

Flask provides a built-in test client that mimics HTTP requests. This allows you to test your endpoints directly from within your application, without having to rely on external tools like Postman or curl. Flask's test client is particularly useful for unit testing, as you can simulate requests and check responses programmatically.

Example of using Flask's test client:

python

Copy

```
import unittest
from app import app

class FlaskTestCase(unittest.TestCase):

    # Setup the Flask test client
    def setUp(self):
        self.app = app.test_client()
        self.app.testing = True

    # Test the GET /api/users endpoint
    def test_get_users(self):
        response = self.app.get('/api/users')
        self.assertEqual(response.status_code, 200)
        self.assertIn('Alice', response.data.decode())

    # Test the POST /api/users endpoint
    def test_create_user(self):
        response = self.app.post('/api/users', json={'name': 'Charlie'})
        self.assertEqual(response.status_code, 201)
        self.assertIn('Charlie', response.data.decode())

if __name__ == '__main__':
    unittest.main()
```

Here's what's happening:

- We use the setUp method to create an instance of the Flask test client. This allows us to simulate HTTP requests.
- The test_get_users method sends a GET request to /api/users and checks that the response status code is 200 OK and that the name "Alice" appears in the response data.
- The test_create_user method sends a POST request to /api/users with a JSON body containing a new user's name and checks that the response status code is 201 Created.

Running Tests

To run the tests, save the file and run it from the terminal:

bash

Copy

```
python -m unittest test_app.py
```

If everything is set up correctly, the tests will run, and you'll get a summary of the results, showing whether each test passed or failed.

Using Postman for Manual Testing

While Flask's test client is great for automated testing, Postman is useful for manual testing and exploring your API. You can send HTTP requests to your Flask server and inspect the responses. With Postman, you can:

- Test GET, POST, PUT, and DELETE requests with different payloads.
- Set request headers, including Content-Type and Authorization.
- Inspect the response body, headers, and status codes.

By combining Flask's built-in testing tools and external tools like Postman, you can ensure that your API behaves as expected under different conditions.

In this chapter, we covered important aspects of building a robust API, including using response codes and status messages, handling errors with Flask's built-in mechanisms, and testing your API locally. Proper response codes and error handling make your API more user-friendly, while thorough testing ensures that your application works reliably and performs well. With these skills in hand, you are now ready to take your Flask API development to the next level by implementing more advanced features like authentication, pagination, and data validation.

Chapter 4: Working with Databases

4.1. Choosing Between Relational and NoSQL Databases

When building an API, one of the most important decisions you'll make is how to store your data. There are two main types of databases to consider: **relational databases** (SQL) and **NoSQL databases.** Both types have their strengths and weaknesses, and the right choice depends on your specific use case and application requirements.

Relational Databases (SQL)

Relational databases, like **PostgreSQL**, **MySQL**, and **SQLite**, store data in tables with predefined schemas. These databases use **Structured Query Language (SQL)** to manage and query the data. They are ideal for applications that require **data consistency**, **ACID properties** (Atomicity, Consistency, Isolation, Durability), and **complex queries** (e.g., JOIN operations across multiple tables).

Key Features of Relational Databases:

- **Structured Data**: Data is stored in tables with rows and columns, and each table typically represents a specific type of entity (e.g., users, orders, products).
- **Normalization**: Data is often normalized, meaning redundant data is minimized and relationships between different entities are explicitly defined (e.g., foreign keys).
- **SQL Queries**: SQL is used to perform complex queries, including joins, filtering, and aggregation.
- **Transactions**: Relational databases support transactional operations, ensuring that all changes are consistent and atomic.

When to Use Relational Databases:

- When your application requires complex relationships between entities (e.g., many-to-many, one-to-many).
- When you need ACID compliance to ensure data integrity.
- When your data structure is well-defined and unlikely to change frequently.
- When you need to perform complex queries that involve multiple tables or aggregations.

NoSQL Databases

NoSQL databases, like **MongoDB**, **Cassandra**, and **Redis**, are designed to handle unstructured, semi-structured, or flexible data. NoSQL databases are typically schema-less, meaning that data can be stored without predefined structures. They provide more flexibility when working with complex or rapidly changing data, and they scale well horizontally, making them suitable for applications that handle large volumes of unstructured data.

Key Features of NoSQL Databases:

- **Schema-less Data**: NoSQL databases allow you to store data without a fixed schema, making it easy to adapt to changing requirements.
- **Scalability**: NoSQL databases are often designed to scale horizontally, meaning you can add more nodes to handle increased traffic and data volume.
- **Flexible Data Models**: Data can be stored as key-value pairs, documents (JSON-like), or graphs, depending on the specific NoSQL database.
- **Eventual Consistency**: Many NoSQL databases sacrifice strict consistency for improved scalability and performance, offering eventual consistency instead.

When to Use NoSQL Databases:

- When your data is unstructured or semi-structured (e.g., documents, logs, or user-generated content).
- When you need horizontal scalability to handle large amounts of traffic or data.
- When you anticipate frequent changes to your data schema.
- When you need fast read and write performance at scale, often at the expense of consistency.

How to Choose Between Relational and NoSQL Databases

- **Data Model**: If your data can be easily represented in tables with relationships, a relational database is usually the best choice. If your data is semi-structured or flexible (e.g., JSON documents or key-value pairs), a NoSQL database might be more appropriate.
- **Complexity**: Relational databases excel at complex queries involving multiple tables. If your application requires complex relationships and transactions, a relational database is likely the better option.
- **Scalability**: If your application is expected to scale horizontally and handle large amounts of data or traffic, a NoSQL database might be a better fit due to its ability to scale easily.

Both types of databases have their strengths, and the choice largely depends on the nature of your application and your data.

4.2. Setting Up SQLAlchemy with Flask

Once you've chosen a relational database for your Flask application, you'll need a way to interact with that database. **SQLAlchemy** is a powerful and flexible Object Relational

Mapper (ORM) for Python, and it integrates seamlessly with Flask to help you interact with relational databases using Python objects.

Installing SQLAlchemy

To get started with SQLAlchemy, you need to install both **Flask-SQLAlchemy** (the Flask extension for SQLAlchemy) and the database driver for your chosen database (e.g., **psycopg2** for PostgreSQL or **mysql-connector-python** for MySQL).

To install Flask-SQLAlchemy and a database driver, run the following:

bash

Copy

```
pip install Flask-SQLAlchemy psycopg2  # For PostgreSQL
```

Configuring Flask-SQLAlchemy

To use SQLAlchemy in your Flask app, you'll need to configure the database URI and initialize SQLAlchemy. The database URI is a connection string that tells SQLAlchemy where your database is located.

Here's how to set up SQLAlchemy in your Flask app:

1. **Define your configuration in** `config.py`**:**

python

Copy

```
import os

class Config:
   SQLALCHEMY_TRACK_MODIFICATIONS = False  # Disable
Flask-SQLAlchemy event system
```

```
    SQLALCHEMY_DATABASE_URI = os.getenv('DATABASE_URL')  # Set this to your database URL
```

The SQLALCHEMY_DATABASE_URI is the connection string that defines how Flask should connect to your database. For PostgreSQL, it might look something like this:

bash

Copy

```
postgresql://username:password@localhost/mydatabase
```

2. **Initialize SQLAlchemy in app.py:**

python

Copy

```
from flask import Flask
from flask_sqlalchemy import SQLAlchemy

app = Flask(__name__)
app.config.from_object('config.Config')  # Load the configuration
db = SQLAlchemy(app)

if __name__ == '__main__':
    app.run(debug=True)
```

In this setup:

- We load the configuration from the config.py file.
- The db = SQLAlchemy(app) line initializes SQLAlchemy with the Flask app.

Defining Models with SQLAlchemy

Once SQLAlchemy is set up, you can define your database models using Python classes. Each class represents a table in the database, and each instance of the class represents a row in that table.

Example of defining a User model:

python

Copy

```
class User(db.Model):
    id = db.Column(db.Integer, primary_key=True)
    name = db.Column(db.String(100), nullable=False)
    email = db.Column(db.String(100), unique=True, nullable=False)

    def __repr__(self):
        return f'<User {self.name}>'
```

In this example:

- db.Model is the base class for all models.
- id, name, and email are columns in the User table. db.Column defines the type and properties of the column.
- primary_key=True ensures that the id column is the primary key.
- nullable=False means that the column cannot be left empty.

Creating the Database

To create the database tables from your models, run the following commands in a Python shell:

python

Copy

```
from app import db
db.create_all()  # Creates all tables defined in the models
```

This command will create the users table based on the User model. If you want to reset the database, you can drop the tables and create them again.

4.3. Defining Models and Migrations with Flask-Migrate

While defining models with SQLAlchemy is straightforward, database schema changes (like adding new columns or tables) often require migrations. Flask-Migrate is an extension that handles database migrations using **Alembic**, which is built on top of SQLAlchemy.

Installing Flask-Migrate

To use Flask-Migrate, install it along with Flask-SQLAlchemy:

bash

Copy

```
pip install Flask-Migrate
```

Setting Up Flask-Migrate

1. **Initialize Flask-Migrate in app.py:**

python

Copy

```
from flask_migrate import Migrate
```

```
migrate = Migrate(app, db)  # Bind Migrate to the app and db
```

2. **Initialize the Migration Repository:**

Run the following command to initialize the migration repository:

bash

Copy

```
flask db init
```

This command creates a migrations folder where all migration files will be stored.

Creating a Migration

Whenever you make changes to your models (e.g., adding a new column), you need to generate a migration. Run this command to create a new migration file:

bash

Copy

```
flask db migrate -m "Add email column to users table"
```

This command will generate a migration script that describes the changes made to the database schema.

Applying Migrations

Once you've generated a migration, you need to apply it to the database. Run this command to upgrade the database schema:

bash

Copy

```
flask db upgrade
```

This applies the migrations and updates your database schema to match the models in your application.

Downgrading Migrations

If you need to revert a migration (e.g., in case of an error), you can downgrade the database to a previous state:

bash

Copy

```
flask db downgrade
```

Flask-Migrate will handle the reversal of the migration steps, returning the database to its previous state.

We explored the basics of working with databases in Flask, starting with the choice between relational and NoSQL databases. We then covered how to set up and configure **SQLAlchemy** with Flask for interacting with relational databases. Finally, we introduced **Flask-Migrate** for managing database schema changes through migrations. With this foundation, you're now equipped to work with databases in Flask, handling everything from basic CRUD operations to more complex database migrations and schema changes.

4.4. Performing CRUD Operations in Flask APIs

CRUD operations (Create, Read, Update, and Delete) are the basic functions of interacting with a database. Flask, combined with SQLAlchemy (for relational databases) or other libraries, makes it easy to implement these operations for your API. In this section, we'll cover how to perform each of the CRUD operations using Flask and SQLAlchemy.

Creating a New Resource (POST Request)

To create a new resource (i.e., add a new record in the database), you'll typically use a **POST** request. Let's use the User model from the previous example and create a new user.

Example of a **POST** request to create a new user:

python

Copy

```
from flask import Flask, request, jsonify
from flask_sqlalchemy import SQLAlchemy

app = Flask(__name__)
app.config['SQLALCHEMY_DATABASE_URI'] = 'sqlite:///users.db'  # For local
SQLite database
db = SQLAlchemy(app)

class User(db.Model):
    id = db.Column(db.Integer, primary_key=True)
```

```
    name = db.Column(db.String(100), nullable=False)
    email = db.Column(db.String(100), unique=True, nullable=False)

@app.route('/api/users', methods=['POST'])
def create_user():
    data = request.get_json()

    if 'name' not in data or 'email' not in data:
        return jsonify({'error': 'Missing required fields'}), 400

    new_user = User(name=data['name'], email=data['email'])
    db.session.add(new_user)
    db.session.commit()

    return jsonify({'id': new_user.id, 'name': new_user.name, 'email': new_user.email}),
201

if __name__ == '__main__':
    app.run(debug=True)
```

In this example:

- The client sends a **POST** request with a JSON payload containing a name and email.
- We check if both fields are provided. If not, we return a 400 Bad Request error.
- The User instance is created, added to the session, and committed to the database.
- The response includes the new user's details and a 201 Created status code.

Reading Resources (GET Request)

The **GET** method is used to retrieve resources. This could be a single resource or a collection of resources.

Example of a **GET** request to fetch all users:

python

Copy

```
@app.route('/api/users', methods=['GET'])
def get_users():
    users = User.query.all()  # Fetch all users from the database
    return jsonify([{'id': user.id, 'name': user.name, 'email': user.email} for user in users]),
200
```

Here:

- We use User.query.all() to fetch all users from the database.
- The data is returned as a JSON array.

To fetch a specific user by ID, you can modify the route like this:

python

Copy

```
@app.route('/api/users/<int:id>', methods=['GET'])
def get_user(id):
    user = User.query.get(id)
    if user is None:
        return jsonify({'error': 'User not found'}), 404
    return jsonify({'id': user.id, 'name': user.name, 'email': user.email}), 200
```

This example retrieves a user by their unique id. If no user is found, a 404 Not Found error is returned.

Updating Resources (PUT Request)

The **PUT** method is used to update an existing resource. Typically, you'll send the updated data to the server in the request body.

Example of a **PUT** request to update a user:

python

Copy

```
@app.route('/api/users/<int:id>', methods=['PUT'])
def update_user(id):
    user = User.query.get(id)
    if user is None:
        return jsonify({'error': 'User not found'}), 404

    data = request.get_json()
    user.name = data.get('name', user.name)
    user.email = data.get('email', user.email)

    db.session.commit()
    return jsonify({'id': user.id, 'name': user.name, 'email': user.email}), 200
```

In this case:

- We fetch the user by ID, and if the user exists, we update their name and email fields.
- If the fields aren't provided in the request, the old values are retained.

- The database session is committed, and the updated user is returned in the response.

Deleting Resources (DELETE Request)

The **DELETE** method is used to remove a resource from the database.

Example of a **DELETE** request to remove a user:

python

Copy

```
@app.route('/api/users/<int:id>', methods=['DELETE'])
def delete_user(id):
    user = User.query.get(id)
    if user is None:
        return jsonify({'error': 'User not found'}), 404

    db.session.delete(user)
    db.session.commit()

    return jsonify({'message': 'User deleted successfully'}), 200
```

Here:

- We retrieve the user by ID. If the user exists, we delete the user from the session and commit the changes to the database.
- If the user is not found, a 404 Not Found response is returned.

4.5. Working with NoSQL: Integrating MongoDB

While relational databases like SQLAlchemy are great for structured data, many modern applications need to work with unstructured or semi-structured data. For this, **NoSQL** databases like **MongoDB** are often a better choice. MongoDB is a document-oriented NoSQL database that stores data in flexible, JSON-like documents, making it ideal for applications that need to store varied data types or scale horizontally.

Installing Flask-PyMongo

To integrate MongoDB with Flask, you'll need the **Flask-PyMongo** extension, which makes it easier to work with MongoDB.

You can install Flask-PyMongo using pip:

bash

Copy

```
pip install Flask-PyMongo
```

Setting Up Flask with MongoDB

1. **Set up MongoDB URI in your configuration:**

In your `config.py`, define the connection string for MongoDB:

python

Copy

```
class Config:
    MONGO_URI = "mongodb://localhost:27017/mydatabase"  # Replace with your
MongoDB URI
```

2. **Initialize Flask-PyMongo:**

In your app.py, initialize Flask-PyMongo:

python

Copy

```
from flask import Flask, jsonify, request
from flask_pymongo import PyMongo

app = Flask(__name__)
app.config.from_object('config.Config')
mongo = PyMongo(app)

@app.route('/api/users', methods=['POST'])
def create_user():
    data = request.get_json()
    if 'name' not in data or 'email' not in data:
        return jsonify({'error': 'Missing required fields'}), 400

    users_collection = mongo.db.users  # Accessing the 'users' collection in MongoDB
    user_id = users_collection.insert_one(data).inserted_id

    return jsonify({'id': str(user_id), 'name': data['name'], 'email': data['email']}), 201

if __name__ == '__main__':
    app.run(debug=True)
```

In this example:

- We use mongo.db.users to access the users collection in MongoDB.

- insert_one(data) inserts the new user document into the collection, and inserted_id gives us the ID of the newly created user.

Retrieving Data from MongoDB

Fetching data from MongoDB is simple, and you can use methods like find_one() and find() to retrieve documents.

python

Copy

```
@app.route('/api/users/<string:id>', methods=['GET'])
def get_user(id):
    users_collection = mongo.db.users
    user = users_collection.find_one({'_id': ObjectId(id)})
    if not user:
        return jsonify({'error': 'User not found'}), 404
    return jsonify({'id': str(user['_id']), 'name': user['name'], 'email': user['email']}), 200
```

Here:

- find_one({'_id': ObjectId(id)}) searches the database for a user with the specified id.
- MongoDB stores IDs as ObjectId by default, so you need to convert the string id to an ObjectId when querying.

4.6. Best Practices for Database Performance

When working with databases in Flask, ensuring optimal performance is crucial, especially as your application scales. Whether you're using a relational or NoSQL database, there are several strategies you can implement to ensure your API performs well under heavy load.

Best Practices for Relational Databases (SQLAlchemy)

Use Indexing: Indexes improve query performance by allowing the database to quickly locate the rows that match a search criterion. Be sure to index frequently queried fields (e.g., user email, id).

Example:

python

Copy

```
email = db.Column(db.String(100), unique=True, index=True)
```

1. **Optimize Queries**: Avoid writing inefficient queries, such as those that perform unnecessary joins or scan large tables. Use pagination and filters to limit the amount of data returned by queries.

   Example of pagination:

   python

   Copy

   ```
   users = User.query.paginate(page=1, per_page=10)
   ```

2. **Use Connection Pooling**: Connection pooling allows you to reuse database connections instead of creating a new one for every request. This can significantly improve performance when handling many concurrent users.

Avoid N+1 Query Problem: When fetching related objects (e.g., users and their posts), avoid making a query for each object. Instead, use joinedload or subqueryload to fetch related data in a single query.

Example:

python

Copy

```
from sqlalchemy.orm import joinedload
```

```
users = User.query.options(joinedload(User.posts)).all()
```

3. **Best Practices for NoSQL Databases (MongoDB)**

1. **Use Proper Indexing**: Just like in SQL databases, MongoDB performance can benefit from indexing. Be sure to index fields that are frequently used in queries, such as `email` or `user_id`.
2. **Denormalization**: In NoSQL databases, data is often denormalized to reduce the number of joins. This can help improve performance but requires you to handle data consistency manually.
3. **Use Efficient Queries**: MongoDB offers a rich set of query operators, but it's important to write efficient queries. Avoid full collection scans and always use indexes where appropriate.
4. **Limit Document Size**: MongoDB documents can be large, but there is a 16MB limit on document size. If your documents are close to that size, consider breaking them up or using more efficient data storage formats.

In this chapter, we explored how to perform **CRUD** operations in Flask, using both relational databases with **SQLAlchemy** and NoSQL databases like **MongoDB**. We also covered essential best practices for optimizing database performance to ensure your application can scale effectively. By following these guidelines, you can create robust and efficient APIs that interact with both relational and NoSQL databases, meeting the needs of modern web applications.

Chapter 5: Authentication and Security

5.1. Introduction to API Authentication Methods

When developing APIs, securing access to your data and resources is one of the most important considerations. APIs are often used to expose sensitive data and allow third-party services to interact with your backend systems. Authentication is the process of verifying the identity of users or clients that are making requests to your API. In this chapter, we'll cover different authentication methods, including basic authentication and OAuth, two widely used approaches in API development.

Why Authentication is Crucial

Authentication ensures that only authorized users can access your resources. This is especially important for protecting sensitive user data, managing access levels, and preventing malicious users from exploiting vulnerabilities in your system. Additionally, API security helps prevent **unauthorized access**, **data theft**, and **denial of service** attacks, ensuring your application's integrity.

Common Authentication Methods

There are several ways to authenticate users in an API, but the most commonly used methods are:

1. **Basic Authentication**:
   - Basic Authentication is one of the simplest forms of HTTP authentication. It involves sending a username and password in the request header. The server verifies these credentials, and if valid, grants access to the resource.

- Basic Authentication is usually not recommended for production applications, as sending credentials in plain text can be insecure, especially if the connection is not encrypted using HTTPS.

2. **Token-Based Authentication**:
   - Token-based authentication involves the use of tokens (like **JWTs** or **API tokens**) that are issued to authenticated users. These tokens are then sent in the HTTP headers for each subsequent request.
   - This method is much more secure than Basic Authentication, as it avoids transmitting sensitive information like passwords with every request.
3. **OAuth (Open Authorization)**:
   - OAuth is a more complex and secure authentication method that allows third-party applications to access user resources without exposing the user's credentials. OAuth uses tokens that are obtained through a series of steps, and it supports scopes and permissions, allowing fine-grained access control.
4. **API Keys**:
   - An API key is a simple authentication mechanism in which a client sends a unique key in the request header to identify itself. This method is often used for server-to-server communication or for public APIs, but it may not offer the same level of security as OAuth or token-based systems.

In this chapter, we will focus on two widely used authentication methods: **Basic Authentication** and **OAuth**.

5.2. Implementing Basic Authentication in Flask

Basic Authentication is a simple method where the client sends the username and password in the request header, encoded in Base64. This method is straightforward to implement, but it should only be used in secure environments (over HTTPS) to protect the credentials from being exposed in transit.

Setting Up Basic Authentication in Flask

You can implement Basic Authentication in Flask using the Flask-HTTPAuth extension, which simplifies adding authentication to your routes.

Install Flask-HTTPAuth:

To get started, install the Flask-HTTPAuth package:

bash

Copy

```
pip install Flask-HTTPAuth
```

1. **Set Up Basic Authentication**:

   In the example below, we'll create a simple user database (using a dictionary for simplicity) and use Basic Authentication to secure access to an endpoint.

   python

   Copy

```
from flask import Flask, jsonify

from flask_httpauth import HTTPBasicAuth


app = Flask(__name__)
auth = HTTPBasicAuth()


# Simple user data (in a real app, this would be stored in a database)
users = {
    "admin": "password123",
    "guest": "guestpassword"
}
```

```
# Function to verify users
@auth.verify_password
def verify_password(username, password):
    if username in users and users[username] == password:
        return username
    return None

# Secured route with Basic Authentication
@app.route('/api/secure-data')
@auth.login_required
def get_secure_data():
    return jsonify({"message": "This is protected data!", "user": auth.current_user()})

if __name__ == '__main__':
    app.run(debug=True)
```

In this example:

- We import and initialize the HTTPBasicAuth object.
- A simple dictionary users is used to store the username-password pairs.
- The verify_password function checks if the provided username and password match the data in the dictionary.
- The @auth.login_required decorator is applied to the /api/secure-data route, which means this route will require authentication.

How It Works:

- When the client sends a request to /api/secure-data, the server expects the request to contain the Authorization header with the value Basic <Base64(username:password)>.

- The verify_password function checks the credentials, and if they match, the request proceeds. If not, Flask will automatically return a 401 Unauthorized response.

Testing Basic Authentication

To test the endpoint, use a tool like **Postman** or **curl** to make a request with the correct Authorization header.

Example with curl:

bash

Copy

```
curl -u admin:password123 http://127.0.0.1:5000/api/secure-data
```

This sends the username and password in the Authorization header, and if the credentials are correct, you'll receive the protected data.

5.3. Using OAuth for Secure Authentication

OAuth (Open Authorization) is a widely-used, secure, and flexible authentication framework. It allows third-party applications to access user resources without exposing the user's credentials, making it ideal for scenarios where users log in via third-party services like **Google**, **Facebook**, or **GitHub**.

OAuth involves a more complex flow compared to Basic Authentication, but it is much more secure because it does not require the transmission of user credentials directly. Instead, OAuth uses **access tokens** to grant access to specific resources.

OAuth Flow Overview

OAuth typically works in two main flows:

- **Authorization Code Flow**: Used by web applications, where the user is redirected to an OAuth provider (like Google) to grant access, and the provider returns an authorization code that the client exchanges for an access token.
- **Implicit Flow**: Used by client-side (JavaScript) applications where tokens are directly returned after authentication, without an intermediate authorization code.

For the sake of simplicity, we'll focus on the **Authorization Code Flow**, which is more suitable for server-side applications.

Setting Up OAuth with Flask

To implement OAuth in Flask, you can use the Flask-OAuthlib extension or the more modern **Authlib** library. Let's go through a basic example of using **Authlib** for OAuth authentication.

1. **Install Authlib**:

bash

Copy

```
pip install Authlib
```

2. **OAuth Setup with Flask**:

Here's an example of how to implement OAuth with Google for authentication:

python

Copy

```
from flask import Flask, redirect, url_for, session
```

```
from authlib.integrations.flask_client import OAuth

app = Flask(__name__)
app.secret_key = 'randomsecretkey'  # Use a strong secret key for production
oauth = OAuth(app)

# Configure Google OAuth
google = oauth.register(
    'google',
    client_id='YOUR_GOOGLE_CLIENT_ID',
    client_secret='YOUR_GOOGLE_CLIENT_SECRET',
    authorize_url='https://accounts.google.com/o/oauth2/auth',
    authorize_params=None,
    access_token_url='https://accounts.google.com/o/oauth2/token',
    refresh_token_url=None,
    client_kwargs={'scope': 'openid profile email'},
)

@app.route('/')
def homepage():
    return 'Welcome to the Flask OAuth example!'

@app.route('/login')
def login():
    # Redirect to Google for login
    redirect_uri = url_for('auth', _external=True)
    return google.authorize_redirect(redirect_uri)

@app.route('/auth')
```

```
def auth():
    # Get the authorization response and fetch the access token
    google.authorize_access_token()
    user = google.parse_id_token()
    session['user'] = user
    return redirect('/dashboard')

@app.route('/dashboard')
def dashboard():
    # Display user information from session
    user = session.get('user')
    if user:
        return f'Hello, {user["name"]}!'
    return redirect(url_for('login'))

if __name__ == '__main__':
    app.run(debug=True)
```

In this example:

- We set up the OAuth client with Google's OAuth configuration. You'll need to register your app with Google and get the client_id and client_secret.
- The /login route redirects the user to Google for authentication.
- Once the user grants access, they are redirected to the /auth route, where the access token is retrieved and stored in the session.
- The /dashboard route shows the user's profile data if they are logged in.

OAuth with Other Providers

The setup for other providers, like GitHub, Facebook, or Twitter, is similar. Each provider will have specific configurations and API endpoints, but the general OAuth flow remains the same: the client redirects the user to the provider, receives an authorization code, exchanges it for an access token, and then uses that token to access the user's resources.

We covered two common authentication methods for Flask APIs: **Basic Authentication** and **OAuth**. We implemented Basic Authentication using the Flask-HTTPAuth extension, which provides a simple way to authenticate users by verifying their username and password. We also explored how to integrate **OAuth** for secure authentication using third-party providers like Google, enabling users to authenticate without exposing their credentials. By understanding and implementing these authentication methods, you can ensure your Flask API is secure and that users can safely access protected resources.

5.4. JSON Web Tokens (JWT) for Stateless Authentication

As your API scales and more users interact with it, **stateless authentication** becomes increasingly important. Traditional session-based authentication involves maintaining user state on the server side, but this can be cumbersome and not ideal for APIs, where clients (such as mobile apps or third-party services) might interact with your backend. This is where **JSON Web Tokens (JWT)** come in as a lightweight, stateless alternative for user authentication.

What are JSON Web Tokens (JWT)?

A **JSON Web Token (JWT)** is a compact, URL-safe token format that is used for securely transmitting information between parties. It contains a set of claims (information) that are encoded and signed. In the context of API authentication, JWTs are used to verify the identity of users and to ensure that the user is authorized to access certain resources.

The JWT format consists of three parts:

1. **Header**: Typically contains the type of token (JWT) and the signing algorithm (e.g., HS256).
2. **Payload**: Contains the claims or information (such as the user's ID, email, and roles). This is the part of the JWT that is not encrypted, so it should not contain sensitive data.
3. **Signature**: This is used to verify that the token was issued by a trusted source and that the token has not been tampered with. It is created by signing the header and payload using a secret key or public/private key pair.

JWTs are typically sent in the Authorization header of HTTP requests, which makes them ideal for stateless APIs.

How JWTs Work in Flask

To implement JWT authentication in Flask, we'll use the pyjwt package to handle token creation and verification.

Install PyJWT:
To get started, install the pyjwt package:

bash

Copy

```
pip install pyjwt
```

1. **Generating JWTs**:
   After a user successfully logs in, the server generates a JWT, which is then sent back to the client. The client will store this token (typically in local storage or

cookies) and include it in subsequent requests to authenticate the user.

Example of generating a JWT in Flask:

python

Copy

```
import jwt

import datetime

from flask import Flask, jsonify, request

from functools import wraps


app = Flask(__name__)

app.config['SECRET_KEY'] = 'your_secret_key_here'  # Use a secure key in production


# Function to create JWT

def create_token(user_id):

    payload = {

        'user_id': user_id,

        'exp': datetime.datetime.utcnow() + datetime.timedelta(hours=1)  # Expiration time

    }

    token = jwt.encode(payload, app.config['SECRET_KEY'], algorithm='HS256')

    return token
```

```
# Protecting routes with JWT authentication
def token_required(f):
    @wraps(f)
    def decorator(*args, **kwargs):
        token = None
        if 'Authorization' in request.headers:
            token = request.headers['Authorization'].split(' ')[1]

        if not token:
            return jsonify({'message': 'Token is missing!'}), 401

        try:
            # Decode the token to verify its validity
            data = jwt.decode(token, app.config['SECRET_KEY'], algorithms=['HS256'])
            current_user_id = data['user_id']
        except Exception as e:
            return jsonify({'message': 'Token is invalid!'}), 401
```

```
        return f(current_user_id, *args, **kwargs)

    return decorator

# Route that generates a token upon successful login
@app.route('/login', methods=['POST'])
def login():
    # Assuming the user credentials are correct
    user_id = request.json.get('user_id')
    token = create_token(user_id)
    return jsonify({'token': token})

# A protected route that requires a valid JWT token
@app.route('/dashboard', methods=['GET'])
@token_required
def dashboard(current_user_id):
    return jsonify({'message': f'Welcome User {current_user_id}!'})

if __name__ == '__main__':
```

```
app.run(debug=True)
```

2. In this example:
    - **Creating a JWT**: The create_token() function creates a JWT with the user_id in the payload and sets an expiration time (1 hour in this case).
    - **Protecting routes**: The token_required() decorator is used to protect routes. It checks the request header for a token, validates it, and allows access to the route only if the token is valid.
    - **Login Route**: The /login route generates a JWT when the user submits valid credentials (e.g., username and password).

Sending the JWT with Requests:
The client must send the JWT in the Authorization header of requests:

bash

Copy

```
curl -H "Authorization: Bearer <your_jwt_token>" http://127.0.0.1:5000/dashboard
```

3. If the token is valid, the server will allow access to the /dashboard route; otherwise, it will return a 401 Unauthorized response.

5.5. CORS (Cross-Origin Resource Sharing) and Flask

When your Flask API is accessed from a different domain (for example, a frontend application hosted on a different server), you may encounter issues related to **Cross-Origin Resource Sharing (CORS)**. CORS is a security feature implemented by web browsers to prevent malicious websites from making unauthorized requests to a server. However, in some cases, you may want to allow cross-origin requests from trusted domains (e.g., your frontend application).

What is CORS?

CORS is a mechanism that allows servers to specify which domains are permitted to access their resources. When a browser sends a request to a server hosted on a different domain, it includes an Origin header, and the server must respond with the appropriate CORS headers (Access-Control-Allow-Origin) to indicate that the request is allowed.

Enabling CORS in Flask

To enable CORS in Flask, you can use the flask-cors extension, which makes it easy to manage cross-origin requests.

Install Flask-CORS:
Install the Flask-CORS extension:
bash
Copy
```
pip install flask-cors
```

1. **Configuring CORS in Flask**:
   Once Flask-CORS is installed, you can configure it to allow cross-origin requests from specific domains or to enable CORS for all domains.
   Example of enabling CORS for all routes:
   python
   Copy
   ```
   from flask import Flask, jsonify
   ```

```
from flask_cors import CORS
```

```python
app = Flask(__name__)

CORS(app)  # Enable CORS for all routes and all domains



@app.route('/api/data')

def get_data():

    return jsonify({'message': 'This is data from Flask API'})



if __name__ == '__main__':

    app.run(debug=True)
```

2. In this example:
   - The CORS(app) call enables CORS for all routes and accepts requests from any origin.
   - You can also specify more granular CORS settings, such as allowing only specific domains or limiting allowed methods and headers.

Allowing Specific Origins:
You can limit CORS to specific origins by passing the origins parameter to the CORS() function.
Example:
python
Copy

```python
CORS(app, origins=["http://localhost:3000", "https://your-frontend-domain.com"])
```

3. This ensures that only requests from http://localhost:3000 and https://your-frontend-domain.com are allowed.

5.6. Preventing Common Security Vulnerabilities (SQL Injection, XSS, CSRF)

When developing APIs, it's important to protect against common security vulnerabilities that can be exploited by malicious users. These vulnerabilities include **SQL injection**, **Cross-Site Scripting (XSS)**, and **Cross-Site Request Forgery (CSRF)**. Let's look at how to prevent each of these in your Flask API.

1. SQL Injection:

SQL injection occurs when an attacker manipulates an SQL query by injecting malicious SQL code through user input. This can lead to unauthorized access to your database, data leaks, and data corruption.

How to prevent SQL Injection:

- **Use Parameterized Queries**: Always use parameterized queries or ORM methods (like SQLAlchemy) to interact with the database. This ensures that user inputs are treated as data and not part of the SQL query.

Example with SQLAlchemy (safe):

python

Copy

```
user = db.session.query(User).filter_by(email=email).first()
```

Using SQLAlchemy's ORM methods automatically escapes user input, preventing SQL injection.

2. Cross-Site Scripting (XSS):

XSS occurs when an attacker injects malicious scripts into web pages, which are then executed by unsuspecting users' browsers. This can lead to stealing user data or performing actions on behalf of the user.

How to prevent XSS:

- **Escape User Inputs**: Always sanitize or escape user-generated content to ensure that any potentially dangerous code (like JavaScript) is not executed in the user's browser.
- **Use Content Security Policy (CSP)**: Implement CSP headers to restrict the types of scripts that can be executed on your site.

In Flask, you can use the html module to escape user input:

python

Copy

```
from html import escape


@app.route('/submit', methods=['POST'])

def submit():

    user_input = request.form['input']

    safe_input = escape(user_input)  # Escape HTML
```

```
return render_template('response.html', user_input=safe_input)
```

3. Cross-Site Request Forgery (CSRF):

CSRF is an attack where a malicious user tricks a logged-in user into making an unwanted request to a site with the user's credentials. This can lead to unwanted actions, such as transferring money or changing account details.

How to prevent CSRF:

- **Use Anti-CSRF Tokens**: Anti-CSRF tokens are unique tokens that are generated for each request and must be included in forms or headers. This ensures that the request is coming from a trusted source.
- **Enable CSRF Protection**: Flask has a built-in CSRF protection feature in Flask-WTF (for forms) and Flask-SeaSurf (for APIs).

Example with Flask-WTF:

bash

Copy

```
pip install flask-wtf
```

Then, in your app:

python

Copy

```
from flask_wtf.csrf import CSRFProtect

csrf = CSRFProtect(app)
```

This will enable CSRF protection for all POST requests by ensuring that each request contains a valid CSRF token.

In this chapter, we covered several important aspects of API security, including **JWT** for stateless authentication, **CORS** for managing cross-origin requests, and common vulnerabilities like **SQL injection**, **XSS**, and **CSRF**. By implementing the appropriate security practices and using secure authentication methods, you can protect your Flask APIs from malicious attacks and ensure that only authorized users can access your resources. These measures are essential for building secure and reliable APIs.

Chapter 6: Flask Performance Optimization

6.1. Introduction to API Performance Metrics

As your Flask API grows and is used by more clients, **performance optimization** becomes crucial for providing a smooth and efficient user experience. Performance can be affected by various factors, including how quickly your API responds, how well your database performs, and how efficiently your server handles concurrent requests.

API performance metrics are used to measure and track the efficiency of your API. Monitoring these metrics helps you identify bottlenecks and areas for improvement. Here are the key performance metrics that are important for evaluating and optimizing your Flask API:

Key Performance Metrics:

1. **Response Time**:
   - **Definition**: The time it takes for the server to respond to a client request, typically measured in milliseconds (ms). Shorter response times result in a better user experience.
   - **How to Measure**: You can track response times at the API level using tools like Flask-Logging or external services like **New Relic** or **Datadog**.
2. **Throughput**:
   - **Definition**: The number of requests that your API can handle within a given period (e.g., requests per second or requests per minute).
   - **How to Measure**: You can monitor throughput using server logs, or tools like **Prometheus** and **Grafana** for real-time monitoring.

3. **Error Rate**:
    - **Definition**: The percentage of requests that result in errors (e.g., 500 Internal Server Error, 404 Not Found). A high error rate could indicate issues with your API or its infrastructure.
    - **How to Measure**: Monitor error responses and track HTTP status codes to get insights into your error rate.
4. **Latency**:
    - **Definition**: Latency refers to the delay between sending a request and receiving a response. High latency can be caused by various factors, including slow database queries or network issues.
    - **How to Measure**: Latency can be measured by calculating the time difference between when a request is made and when the response is received.
5. **Resource Utilization**:
    - **Definition**: The CPU, memory, and disk usage of your application and server during operation. High resource consumption can slow down your API and cause scalability issues.
    - **How to Measure**: Tools like **htop**, **top**, or **Prometheus** can be used to monitor system resource usage.

By regularly measuring and tracking these metrics, you can identify performance bottlenecks, assess where optimizations are necessary, and take appropriate actions to improve your API's efficiency and scalability.

6.2. Reducing Response Time with Caching

One of the most effective ways to improve the performance of your API is by reducing **response time**. **Caching** is a technique that involves storing frequently accessed data temporarily so that future requests can retrieve it quickly without needing to process it again. Caching can drastically reduce response times, especially for read-heavy APIs, and improve overall system performance.

Why Caching Improves Performance

- **Reduce Load on Server and Database**: By caching the results of frequent queries or operations, you reduce the need to hit the database or perform expensive calculations every time a request is made.
- **Faster Responses**: Cached data can be retrieved much faster than querying the database or performing a computation.
- **Scalability**: Caching helps to offload the server and database, making your API more scalable under high traffic.

Types of Caching

1. **In-Memory Caching**:
   - In-memory caches store data in the server's memory (RAM). This is extremely fast because accessing memory is much quicker than querying a database.
   - Common in-memory caching systems include **Redis** and **Memcached**.
2. **HTTP Caching**:
   - HTTP caching is used to cache the responses of API requests. This can be done at the client-side (in the browser) or at the server-side (using a reverse proxy like **Varnish** or **NGINX**).
   - HTTP headers like Cache-Control, ETag, and Expires are used to control caching behavior.

3. **Database Query Caching**:
    - Query caching stores the results of frequent database queries so that subsequent requests don't need to execute the query again. This can be particularly useful for expensive database operations.
    - Flask itself doesn't have built-in query caching, but you can use **Flask-Caching** to implement caching for routes or specific operations.

Implementing Caching in Flask

The **Flask-Caching** extension provides an easy way to implement caching in your Flask app. You can cache the results of entire routes or specific function calls.

Install Flask-Caching:

bash

Copy

```
pip install Flask-Caching
```

1. **Set Up Flask-Caching**:

   Here's how to set up Flask-Caching with **Redis**:

   python

   Copy

```
from flask import Flask, jsonify

from flask_caching import Cache


app = Flask(__name__)
app.config['CACHE_TYPE'] = 'redis'  # Use Redis for caching
app.config['CACHE_DEFAULT_TIMEOUT'] = 300  # Cache timeout in seconds


cache = Cache(app)
```

```
@app.route('/api/data')
@cache.cached()  # Cache the result of this route
def get_data():
    # Simulate a slow function (e.g., a database query)
    data = {'message': 'This is data from the server'}
    return jsonify(data)

if __name__ == '__main__':
    app.run(debug=True)
```

2. In this example:
   - Flask-Caching is initialized with the Redis cache type.
   - The @cache.cached() decorator is applied to the /api/data route, which caches the result of the route for 5 minutes.
   - If the route is accessed again within the cache timeout, the result is served from the cache instead of recalculating or querying the database.
3. **Invalidating Cache**:
   - Sometimes, you might need to clear or invalidate the cache manually (e.g., when data changes). Flask-Caching provides methods to do this:

python

Copy

```
cache.delete('key')  # Delete specific cache
cache.clear()  # Clear all cached data
```

4. Caching can also be set up for database queries by using Flask-Caching's **@cache.cached()** decorator on database routes or queries.

Best Practices for Caching:

- **Cache Expiry**: Set reasonable expiration times for your cache to ensure that data doesn't become stale. For dynamic data, you may want to set shorter timeouts.
- **Cache Only Expensive Operations**: Cache the results of slow database queries, computations, or third-party API calls, but avoid caching dynamic or frequently changing data like user sessions.
- **Use Cache Invalidation**: Ensure that cached data is invalidated or refreshed when data changes (e.g., after updates or deletions).

6.3. Optimizing Database Queries with Indexing

A key factor in improving your API's performance is optimizing how your application interacts with the database. **Database indexing** is one of the most effective ways to speed up query performance. An index is a data structure that helps the database engine find and retrieve rows more efficiently.

How Indexing Works

When you query a database table, the database engine must scan all rows to find matching records. Indexes work by creating a smaller, sorted data structure that enables faster searching. Instead of scanning every row in a table, the database can quickly locate the relevant index entry, which points to the full row in the table.

When to Use Indexing

- **Frequently Queried Columns**: Columns that are frequently used in WHERE, JOIN, ORDER BY, or GROUP BY clauses should be indexed to improve query performance.

- **Foreign Keys**: Foreign key columns (used for relationships between tables) should be indexed to speed up joins.
- **Unique Constraints**: If a column must have unique values (e.g., email or username), indexing it can speed up queries that check for uniqueness.

How to Create Indexes with SQLAlchemy

In SQLAlchemy, you can define indexes directly in your models. Here's how to create an index for a frequently queried column:

python

Copy

```
from flask import Flask
from flask_sqlalchemy import SQLAlchemy

app = Flask(__name__)
app.config['SQLALCHEMY_DATABASE_URI'] = 'sqlite:///mydatabase.db'
db = SQLAlchemy(app)

class User(db.Model):
    id = db.Column(db.Integer, primary_key=True)
    name = db.Column(db.String(100), index=True)  # Index the 'name' column
    email = db.Column(db.String(100), unique=True)  # Automatically indexed due to
'unique=True'

    def __repr__(self):
        return f'<User {self.name}>'

if __name__ == '__main__':
    app.run(debug=True)
```

In this example:

- The name column is indexed using index=True, which speeds up searches that filter by name.
- The email column is unique, and SQLAlchemy automatically creates an index for it.

Querying with Indexes

Once an index is created, you can benefit from faster queries that search, filter, or join on the indexed columns. For example, querying users by name will now be much faster:

python

Copy

```
users = User.query.filter_by(name='Alice').all()  # Optimized with the index
```

Indexing Best Practices

- **Limit the Number of Indexes**: While indexes speed up read queries, they can slow down writes (insert, update, delete operations). Only create indexes on columns that are frequently queried.
- **Use Composite Indexes**: If you often query multiple columns together, consider creating a composite index on those columns. For example, if you frequently filter by both name and email, you can create a combined index.
- **Monitor Index Usage**: Over time, certain indexes may no longer be necessary. Monitor query performance to determine whether any indexes should be removed or adjusted.

We explored key techniques for optimizing Flask API performance. We covered **API performance metrics** that help you track and analyze the performance of your API. We also discussed **caching** as a powerful way to reduce response times and improve scalability. Finally, we examined how **indexing** database queries can speed up data retrieval and improve overall performance. By applying these strategies, you can ensure that your Flask API remains fast, efficient, and scalable as it grows.

6.4. Asynchronous Task Handling with Celery

Handling long-running tasks in Flask can become challenging, especially when these tasks slow down your API's response time. Tasks like sending emails, processing large files, or making external API calls can block the request/response cycle and lead to poor user experiences. This is where **asynchronous task handling** comes in.

Celery is a popular distributed task queue that helps manage asynchronous tasks in Flask. By offloading tasks to Celery workers, you can keep your Flask app responsive while executing time-consuming operations in the background.

How Celery Works

Celery works by managing a queue of tasks that can be executed asynchronously by worker processes. Flask sends the task to a queue, and a worker picks it up for execution. Once the task is complete, the worker can return the result.

Setting Up Celery with Flask

Install Celery and Redis:

First, you need to install **Celery** and a message broker. Redis is a common choice for the message broker.

bash

Copy

```
pip install celery redis
```

1. **Configuring Celery with Flask**:

   Create a new file app.py and set up Celery alongside Flask.

   python

   Copy

```
from flask import Flask, jsonify

from celery import Celery

app = Flask(__name__)

# Configure Celery to use Redis as the message broker
app.config['CELERY_BROKER_URL'] = 'redis://localhost:6379/0'
app.config['CELERY_RESULT_BACKEND'] = 'redis://localhost:6379/0'

celery = Celery(app.name, broker=app.config['CELERY_BROKER_URL'])
celery.conf.update(app.config)

@celery.task
def long_running_task():
    import time
    time.sleep(5)  # Simulate a long-running task
    return 'Task completed'

@app.route('/start-task', methods=['GET'])
def start_task():
    task = long_running_task.apply_async()  # Asynchronously execute the task
    return jsonify({'message': 'Task started', 'task_id': task.id})

@app.route('/check-task/<task_id>', methods=['GET'])
def check_task(task_id):
```

```
    task = long_running_task.AsyncResult(task_id)
    if task.state == 'SUCCESS':
        return jsonify({'task_id': task.id, 'status': 'Completed', 'result': task.result})
    return jsonify({'task_id': task.id, 'status': task.state})

if __name__ == '__main__':
    app.run(debug=True)
```

2. In this setup:
    - We configure Flask to use **Redis** as the message broker.
    - The long_running_task function is decorated with @celery.task, which turns it into a Celery task.
    - The /start-task route triggers the task asynchronously, and /check-task/<task_id> allows the user to check the task's status.

Running Celery Workers:
To start Celery workers, you need to run the following command in a terminal (assuming you have Redis running):

bash

Copy

```
celery -A app.celery worker --loglevel=info
```

3. This starts a worker process that listens for tasks in the Redis queue and processes them asynchronously.
4. **Testing the Asynchronous Task**:
    - Visit http://127.0.0.1:5000/start-task to start the task.
    - Celery will process the task in the background while Flask continues to respond to other requests.
    - Visit http://127.0.0.1:5000/check-task/<task_id> to check the status of the task.

Benefits of Using Celery for Asynchronous Tasks:

- **Non-blocking**: Celery offloads tasks to separate processes, allowing Flask to remain responsive.
- **Scalable**: Celery workers can be scaled horizontally by adding more worker processes.
- **Distributed**: Tasks can be distributed across multiple servers, improving reliability and fault tolerance.

6.5. Profiling and Load Testing Flask APIs

Profiling and **load testing** are essential practices for ensuring that your Flask API performs optimally under varying levels of traffic. Profiling helps identify performance bottlenecks in your code, while load testing simulates real-world usage to measure how your API handles high levels of traffic.

Profiling Flask APIs

Profiling is the process of monitoring the execution time of various parts of your Flask application to identify performance bottlenecks.

Using Flask's Built-In Profiler:
Flask comes with a built-in **profiler** that you can use to measure the execution time of each route. The Flask-DebugToolbar extension also provides useful performance metrics.

Install Flask-DebugToolbar:

bash

Copy

```
pip install flask-debugtoolbar
```

Enable the Debug Toolbar in your app:

python

Copy

```
from flask import Flask
from flask_debugtoolbar import DebugToolbarExtension

app = Flask(__name__)
app.config['DEBUG_TB_INTERCEPT_REDIRECTS'] = False
app.secret_key = 'secret'
toolbar = DebugToolbarExtension(app)

@app.route('/')
def home():
    return "Hello, World!"

if __name__ == '__main__':
    app.run(debug=True)
```

1. The **Flask-DebugToolbar** will display performance information, including SQL queries and request times, on every page of your application.

Using the `cProfile` **Module**:

For more detailed profiling, you can use Python's built-in **cProfile** module. This allows you to track how long each function takes to execute.

Example of profiling using `cProfile`:

python

Copy

```
import cProfile
from flask import Flask
```

```
app = Flask(__name__)

@app.route('/')
def home():
    return "Hello, World!"

if __name__ == '__main__':
    profiler = cProfile.Profile()
    profiler.enable()
    app.run(debug=True)
    profiler.disable()
    profiler.print_stats()
```

2. The cProfile module will log detailed statistics about your app's execution, such as the time spent in each function.

Load Testing Flask APIs

Load testing simulates many users interacting with your API at the same time to test how it performs under stress. There are several tools for load testing Flask APIs, but one of the most common is **Apache JMeter**.

1. **Using Apache JMeter**:
    - JMeter is a popular open-source tool for load testing APIs and websites. You can configure JMeter to send a large number of requests to your Flask API and measure how the system performs.
    - With JMeter, you can simulate multiple users, measure response times, and track performance metrics such as throughput and error rates.

Using locust for Load Testing: locust is another powerful tool for load testing APIs, written in Python. It allows you to define user behavior in Python code and run tests for thousands of simultaneous users.

Install locust:

bash

Copy

```
pip install locust
```

Example locustfile.py:

python

Copy

```
from locust import HttpUser, task, between


class FlaskApiUser(HttpUser):
    wait_time = between(1, 2)


    @task
    def get_home(self):
        self.client.get("/")
```

To run the load test, execute:

bash

Copy

```
locust -f locustfile.py --host=http://127.0.0.1:5000
```

2. This will start Locust, which simulates users accessing the / route and allows you to monitor performance through a web interface.

Key Load Testing Metrics to Measure:

- **Response Time**: Measure the average and peak response times during the load test.

- **Throughput**: Measure how many requests per second your API can handle.
- **Error Rate**: Measure the percentage of requests that fail due to server errors (e.g., 500 errors).
- **Resource Utilization**: Monitor how much CPU and memory your API consumes during load testing.

6.6. Techniques to Handle High Traffic Scenarios

As your API experiences high traffic, it is crucial to implement strategies that ensure the system remains performant and reliable. Here are several techniques for handling high traffic scenarios:

1. Horizontal Scaling (Load Balancing)

Horizontal scaling involves distributing traffic across multiple server instances. This can be achieved through **load balancing**, where a load balancer (like **NGINX** or **HAProxy**) distributes incoming traffic to multiple application servers.

- **Benefits**: Horizontal scaling increases your API's capacity to handle high traffic by adding more server resources.
- **Setup**: Set up multiple instances of your Flask app (e.g., using Docker or virtual machines) and configure a load balancer to distribute requests.

2. Caching Layer (Redis or Memcached)

Using caching layers like **Redis** or **Memcached** helps reduce the load on your database and speeds up data retrieval. For frequently requested resources, such as product listings or user profiles, you can cache the results and serve them from memory.

- **Benefits**: Reduces database load, accelerates response times, and enhances scalability.

- **Setup**: Use tools like **Flask-Caching** or **Flask-Redis** to implement caching in your Flask application.

3. Database Optimization (Sharding, Indexing)

As your API grows, database optimization becomes increasingly important. Implement **indexing** to speed up queries and use **database sharding** to distribute the load across multiple database servers.

- **Sharding**: Break the database into smaller, more manageable pieces by distributing data across multiple servers.
- **Indexing**: Create indexes on frequently queried columns to improve query performance.

4. Rate Limiting

Rate limiting prevents abuse by limiting the number of requests a client can make within a certain timeframe. This can protect your API from being overwhelmed by excessive traffic and prevent service disruptions.

- **Setup**: Use Flask extensions like **Flask-Limiter** to implement rate limiting.

Example of using Flask-Limiter:

bash

Copy

```
pip install Flask-Limiter
```

python

Copy

```
from flask_limiter import Limiter
from flask import Flask
```

```
app = Flask(__name__)
limiter = Limiter(app)

@app.route("/api/endpoint")
@limiter.limit("10 per minute")  # Limit to 10 requests per minute
def api_endpoint():
    return "Request accepted"
```

5. Content Delivery Networks (CDNs)

For static resources (e.g., images, stylesheets, and JavaScript files), use a **Content Delivery Network (CDN)** to serve them. CDNs cache these resources on distributed servers, which reduces the load on your server and speeds up content delivery to users.

In this chapter, we explored various techniques for optimizing Flask API performance. We covered **asynchronous task handling** with Celery, which helps offload long-running tasks to background workers. We also looked at **profiling** and **load testing** to identify and measure performance bottlenecks. Lastly, we discussed strategies for handling **high traffic scenarios**, including **horizontal scaling**, **caching**, and **rate limiting**. By implementing these techniques, you can ensure that your Flask API performs efficiently and remains scalable even under high traffic conditions.

Chapter 7: Building Scalable APIs

7.1. Understanding Horizontal vs. Vertical Scaling

When building scalable APIs, one of the first decisions you need to make is how to scale your application to handle increasing traffic and data. There are two primary approaches to scaling systems: **horizontal scaling** and **vertical scaling**. Both have their own advantages and challenges, and the best approach often depends on the specifics of your application and infrastructure.

What is Vertical Scaling?

Vertical scaling (also known as **scaling up**) involves adding more resources to a single server. This could mean increasing the CPU, RAM, or storage capacity of the existing machine running your application. Vertical scaling is typically easier to implement because it involves upgrading the current server rather than adding new machines.

Advantages of Vertical Scaling:

- **Simplicity**: It's easier to implement since you're only upgrading the existing machine rather than distributing the workload across multiple machines.
- **Cost-Effective for Smaller Applications**: For smaller applications with moderate traffic, scaling vertically may be sufficient and more affordable in the short term.

Challenges of Vertical Scaling:

- **Limited Growth**: There are physical limitations to how much you can scale a single machine. You can only add so much CPU, memory, or storage before you hit a ceiling.

- **Single Point of Failure**: If the server goes down, the entire application becomes unavailable, leading to a potential bottleneck.
- **Not Ideal for High Traffic**: As traffic grows, a single server may struggle to handle the load, resulting in performance degradation.

Use Cases for Vertical Scaling:

- Ideal for applications that don't require extreme levels of concurrency or when there's an immediate need to increase capacity without extensive infrastructure changes.
- Suitable for initial development and small-scale applications.

What is Horizontal Scaling?

Horizontal scaling (also known as **scaling out**) involves adding more machines (or instances) to handle the load. Instead of increasing the capacity of a single server, you distribute the traffic across multiple servers. In modern cloud environments, this often involves adding more instances of your application running behind a **load balancer**.

Advantages of Horizontal Scaling:

- **Better Fault Tolerance**: Since your application is distributed across multiple machines, if one server goes down, others can continue to serve requests. This reduces the risk of a single point of failure.
- **Infinitely Scalable**: You can keep adding servers as needed to handle more traffic. There is no physical limit to how much you can scale horizontally.
- **Improved Performance**: By distributing the load, you can handle a larger volume of requests and ensure the system remains responsive even under high traffic.

Challenges of Horizontal Scaling:

- **Complexity**: Setting up and managing multiple servers can be more complex. You need load balancing, monitoring, and possibly additional components like databases that support scaling (e.g., sharding).
- **Increased Costs**: More servers mean higher infrastructure costs, though this is often offset by the benefits of improved scalability and reliability.

Use Cases for Horizontal Scaling:

- Best suited for applications with unpredictable or high traffic volumes that need to scale quickly.
- Essential for web applications, microservices architectures, and large-scale distributed systems.

Choosing Between Horizontal and Vertical Scaling

The decision to use vertical or horizontal scaling depends on several factors, including:

- **Application Load**: If your application's traffic is predictable and relatively small, vertical scaling might be sufficient. However, if your traffic grows rapidly, horizontal scaling will be more effective.
- **Reliability Requirements**: Horizontal scaling offers better reliability because it distributes traffic across multiple instances, making it more fault-tolerant.
- **Cost Considerations**: Vertical scaling might be more affordable in the short term, but horizontal scaling becomes more cost-effective as traffic and demand grow.

In most modern web applications, **horizontal scaling** is preferred for long-term scalability, but **vertical scaling** can still be a useful strategy for smaller workloads or quick capacity upgrades.

7.2. Scaling Flask Applications Using Load Balancers

Once you decide to scale your Flask application horizontally, you need a way to distribute traffic across multiple server instances. This is where **load balancing** comes into play. A **load balancer** is a system that distributes incoming traffic to multiple servers to ensure that no single server is overwhelmed with too many requests.

What is a Load Balancer?

A load balancer acts as a reverse proxy that sits between the client and your Flask application. It accepts incoming requests from clients and forwards them to one of the available server instances. Load balancers can be configured to distribute traffic in various ways, ensuring efficient resource usage, improved response times, and fault tolerance.

Types of Load Balancing Algorithms

There are several strategies for distributing traffic, including:

1. **Round Robin**:
    - The load balancer forwards each request to the next available server in a circular order.
    - **Use Case**: Simple and works well when the servers have similar capabilities and traffic is evenly distributed.
2. **Least Connections**:
    - The load balancer sends requests to the server with the fewest active connections.
    - **Use Case**: Useful when servers have varying capabilities and load is uneven.

3. **IP Hash**:
    - The load balancer uses the client's IP address to determine which server should handle the request.
    - **Use Case**: When you want to ensure that a client is always directed to the same server, useful for session persistence.
4. **Weighted Round Robin**:
    - Servers with more resources are given a higher weight, meaning they will handle a larger portion of the traffic.
    - **Use Case**: Useful when servers have different capabilities and you want to distribute traffic according to each server's capacity.

Setting Up Load Balancing for Flask

In practice, Flask applications are often deployed behind a reverse proxy server or load balancer like **NGINX**, **HAProxy**, or cloud-based solutions like **AWS Elastic Load Balancing (ELB)** or **Google Cloud Load Balancing**.

Example with NGINX:
To set up load balancing with NGINX, you first need to install and configure NGINX on a separate server (or use it as a proxy if it's already running in a cloud environment). Here's an example NGINX configuration file that load balances traffic between two Flask application instances:

nginx

Copy

```
http {
    upstream flask_app {
        server 127.0.0.1:5000;  # Flask app instance 1
        server 127.0.0.1:5001;  # Flask app instance 2
    }
```

```
    server {
        listen 80;

        location / {
            proxy_pass http://flask_app;
            proxy_set_header Host $host;
            proxy_set_header X-Real-IP $remote_addr;
            proxy_set_header X-Forwarded-For $proxy_add_x_forwarded_for;
        }
    }
}
```

1. In this example:
   - We define an **upstream** block that lists the Flask app instances (127.0.0.1:5000 and 127.0.0.1:5001).
   - The **server** block handles incoming HTTP requests and forwards them to the Flask application instances using the proxy_pass directive.
2. **Testing Load Balancing**:
   Once NGINX is configured, you can start multiple instances of your Flask app (e.g., using **Gunicorn** or **uWSGI**) and test the load balancing behavior by sending requests to the load balancer. You can use tools like **curl**, **Postman**, or **Apache JMeter** for testing.

Handling Sticky Sessions with Load Balancers

In some cases, especially with user authentication or session-based apps, you may need to ensure that requests from the same user are always routed to the same server. This is known as **sticky sessions** or **session affinity**.

You can configure NGINX to handle sticky sessions by using **cookies** or **IP hashing**:

nginx

Copy

```
# Example of sticky session configuration using cookies
upstream flask_app {
   sticky cookie srv_id expires=1h domain=.example.com;
   server 127.0.0.1:5000;
   server 127.0.0.1:5001;
}
```

7.3. Implementing Microservices with Flask

As your application grows, you may find that managing a monolithic application becomes unwieldy. One solution to this is adopting a **microservices architecture**, where your application is broken down into smaller, independently deployable services. Each service handles a specific business function and can be scaled independently.

What are Microservices?

Microservices architecture involves breaking down a large application into smaller services that communicate over APIs. These services are loosely coupled and independently deployable, which makes scaling, development, and maintenance easier.

For example, in an e-commerce application:

- One microservice could handle user authentication.
- Another could manage product catalog.
- Another could handle payment processing.

Each service is typically responsible for a specific part of the application's functionality and communicates with other services over **HTTP** or **message queues**.

Advantages of Microservices:

- **Independent Scaling**: Each service can be scaled independently, so you only need to scale the parts of your app that are under heavy load.
- **Resilience**: If one service fails, the rest of the system can continue functioning.
- **Flexibility in Technology**: Each service can use the best technology suited for its specific requirements.
- **Faster Development**: Smaller, independent services can be developed and deployed more quickly by different teams.

Implementing Microservices with Flask

To implement microservices using Flask, each microservice can be developed as a separate Flask application with its own routes and endpoints. Here's a basic outline of how to structure and implement microservices:

1. **Service 1: User Service**: A Flask app that handles user-related functionality like registration, authentication, and profile management.
2. **Service 2: Product Service**: Another Flask app that manages product listings, pricing, and inventory.
3. **Service 3: Order Service**: A third Flask app that handles order processing and payment.

Each of these services communicates with others using **HTTP APIs** (REST or GraphQL), or more often, **message queues** (e.g., **RabbitMQ** or **Kafka**) for asynchronous communication.

Example of communication between microservices:

python

Copy

```
import requests
```

```
# Assuming Product Service and Order Service are running
response = requests.get('http://product-service/api/products/123')
product = response.json()

# Now send the product data to the Order Service
order_response = requests.post('http://order-service/api/orders', json={'product_id':
product['id']})
```

Managing Microservices with API Gateways

An **API Gateway** acts as a single entry point for all microservices, routing incoming requests to the appropriate service. It can also provide additional functionality, like load balancing, rate limiting, and authentication.

- **Example API Gateway tools**: **Kong**, **NGINX**, **Amazon API Gateway**.

Deploying Microservices

In a microservices architecture, each service is often containerized using **Docker** and orchestrated using a tool like **Kubernetes**. This allows you to manage multiple services, scale them independently, and ensure they are resilient and fault-tolerant.

We explored the concepts of **horizontal vs. vertical scaling**, **load balancing** to distribute traffic across multiple instances, and **implementing microservices** with Flask. We also learned about the key benefits of scaling your application to handle more users and traffic, and how breaking your application into smaller, independent services can improve scalability and resilience. By implementing these strategies, you can ensure that your Flask applications can grow efficiently and handle increased demand without compromising performance or reliability.

7.4. Scaling Database Performance: Sharding and Replication

As your application grows, your database may become a bottleneck. **Scaling the database** is an essential part of building a scalable API, especially when handling large volumes of data and high query traffic. Two common approaches to scaling database performance are **sharding** and **replication**. These techniques help distribute the load and ensure high availability of your data.

Database Sharding

Sharding involves splitting your database into smaller, more manageable pieces, called **shards**, and distributing these shards across multiple servers. Each shard holds a subset of the data, and requests are directed to the appropriate shard based on the data being queried.

For example, in a database with user data, you could shard the database by user ID, where one shard contains users with IDs 1-10000, another contains users 10001-20000, and so on.

Benefits of Sharding:

- **Improved Performance**: Queries are distributed across multiple servers, reducing the load on each server and improving query speed.
- **Scalability**: Sharding allows you to horizontally scale your database by adding more shards as data grows.
- **Fault Isolation**: Since each shard is independent, a failure in one shard won't bring down the entire system.

Challenges of Sharding:

- **Complexity**: Sharding introduces complexity in terms of data distribution, managing multiple shards, and ensuring consistency across them.
- **Cross-Shard Queries**: Queries that need data from multiple shards can be slower because the database must query multiple servers and aggregate the results.

How to Implement Sharding:

1. **Choose a Sharding Strategy**: Common sharding strategies include range-based sharding (e.g., by user ID), hash-based sharding (e.g., by hashing a unique key), or directory-based sharding (using a central directory to decide which shard holds the data).
2. **Database Setup**: Set up your database to support sharding. This might involve configuring **MongoDB** or **Cassandra**, which natively support sharding, or setting up custom sharding logic with traditional relational databases like **MySQL** or **PostgreSQL**.

Database Replication

Replication involves creating copies of your database and distributing them across multiple servers. These copies are known as **replicas**. Replication can improve **read scalability** by offloading read requests to the replicas, while the primary server handles write requests.

There are two types of replication:

1. **Master-Slave Replication**: One primary server (master) handles writes, and multiple read-only replicas (slaves) handle read queries.

2. **Master-Master Replication**: Multiple servers can handle both reads and writes, with data synchronized between them. This setup offers high availability but can lead to consistency challenges.

Benefits of Replication:

- **Improved Read Performance**: Replicas can handle read traffic, reducing the load on the primary server.
- **High Availability**: In case of a failure of the master server, one of the replica servers can be promoted to the master, minimizing downtime.

Challenges of Replication:

- **Consistency**: Keeping data in sync between the primary server and replicas can introduce delays or lead to eventual consistency issues.
- **Write Bottlenecks**: The primary server may become a bottleneck if write-heavy operations dominate, as only the primary server can accept writes.

How to Implement Replication:

1. **Set Up Replication**: Most database systems like **MySQL**, **PostgreSQL**, and **MongoDB** offer built-in support for replication. You can configure your database server to designate one instance as the master and others as replicas.
2. **Load Balancing Reads**: Use a load balancer to distribute read queries between replicas, while write queries continue to be directed to the master.

7.5. Asynchronous Flask with Flask-SocketIO for Real-Time Applications

Asynchronous processing in Flask enables you to handle concurrent tasks efficiently, especially for real-time applications where fast response times are critical. **Flask-SocketIO** is an extension that allows Flask to handle **WebSockets** and other asynchronous communication protocols, enabling real-time bidirectional communication between the client and the server.

What is Flask-SocketIO?

Flask-SocketIO is an extension that integrates **Socket.IO** with Flask, allowing for real-time communication between the server and the client. Socket.IO is a protocol that enables WebSocket-like behavior, which provides low-latency, full-duplex communication over a single, persistent connection.

Use Cases for Flask-SocketIO:

- **Real-Time Chat Applications**: Users can send messages instantly, and others can receive them without waiting for a page reload.
- **Live Notifications**: Users can receive real-time updates about events, messages, or status changes.
- **Collaborative Applications**: Multiple users can interact and update the same data in real time (e.g., live collaboration on a document).

Setting Up Flask-SocketIO

Install Flask-SocketIO:

To use Flask-SocketIO, you need to install it alongside **Flask**.

bash

Copy

```
pip install flask-socketio
```

1. **Setting Up a Basic Flask-SocketIO Example**:
   Here's a simple example of how to set up Flask with Socket.IO to handle real-time communication.
   python
   Copy

```
from flask import Flask, render_template

from flask_socketio import SocketIO, send


app = Flask(__name__)
socketio = SocketIO(app)


@app.route('/')
def index():
    return render_template('index.html')


@socketio.on('message')
def handle_message(message):
    print(f'Received message: {message}')
    send(message, broadcast=True)


if __name__ == '__main__':
    socketio.run(app)
```

2. In this example:
   - The SocketIO object is initialized and tied to the Flask app.
   - The @socketio.on('message') decorator listens for messages from clients, handles them, and broadcasts the same message to all connected clients.

Creating the Client-Side Socket.IO Code:

On the client side, you need to include the **Socket.IO client** library in your HTML file to establish a connection to the Flask server.

html

Copy

```
<!DOCTYPE html>
<html lang="en">
<head>
    <meta charset="UTF-8">
    <title>Socket.IO Chat</title>
    <script src="https://cdn.socket.io/4.0.1/socket.io.min.js"></script>
</head>
<body>
    <input id="message_input" type="text" placeholder="Type a message...">
    <button onclick="sendMessage()">Send</button>
    <ul id="messages"></ul>

    <script>
        const socket = io.connect('http://' + document.domain + ':' + location.port);

        socket.on('message', function(data) {
            const messages = document.getElementById('messages');
            const newMessage = document.createElement('li');
            newMessage.textContent = data;
            messages.appendChild(newMessage);
        });

        function sendMessage() {
            const message = document.getElementById('message_input').value;
```

```
        socket.send(message);
    }
  </script>
</body>
</html>
```

3. In this example:
    - The client connects to the Flask server using socket.connect().
    - When a message is sent by a client, the sendMessage function sends it via the WebSocket connection.
    - All messages sent from the server are broadcast to all clients connected to the same room or channel.
4. **Running the Flask-SocketIO Application**:
   Run the Flask application, and open multiple browser tabs to see real-time communication in action. Messages sent by one client will instantly appear in all other clients connected to the same server.

Benefits of Using Flask-SocketIO:

- **Real-Time Interaction**: Enables real-time, two-way communication between clients and servers, improving user experience for applications like chats or live notifications.
- **Efficient Resource Usage**: WebSockets maintain a persistent connection, reducing the overhead of making multiple HTTP requests.

Challenges of Using Flask-SocketIO:

- **Concurrency**: Flask by default is synchronous, but with Flask-SocketIO, you'll need to use a proper asynchronous server like **eventlet** or **gevent** to handle concurrent clients effectively.

7.6. Using Caching to Enhance Scalability

Caching is an essential technique to enhance scalability and performance by reducing the time it takes to retrieve data. By storing frequently accessed data in memory, caching prevents repetitive and costly operations, such as database queries, from being executed multiple times.

Types of Caching to Improve Scalability:

1. **In-Memory Caching**:
   - **Redis** or **Memcached** are often used to cache frequently accessed data in memory. In-memory caching is much faster than querying a database.
   - Use **Flask-Caching** or **Flask-Redis** to integrate in-memory caching with your Flask application.
2. **Database Query Caching**:
   - Cache the results of frequently run database queries, reducing the load on the database. This can be done at the application level using Flask extensions or at the database level (e.g., MySQL query caching).
3. **HTTP Caching**:
   - For static or semi-static content, HTTP caching headers (`Cache-Control`, `ETag`, etc.) can instruct browsers or intermediary caches to store the response, reducing the need for repeated requests.

Example of Using Redis with Flask Caching:

Install Flask-Caching and Flask-Redis:

bash

Copy

```
pip install Flask-Caching Flask-Redis
```

1. **Configure Redis Caching in Flask**:

   python

Copy

```
from flask import Flask, jsonify

from flask_caching import Cache

app = Flask(__name__)
app.config['CACHE_TYPE'] = 'redis'
app.config['CACHE_REDIS_URL'] = "redis://localhost:6379/0"
cache = Cache(app)

@app.route('/api/data')
@cache.cached(timeout=60)  # Cache this route for 60 seconds
def get_data():
    # Simulate a slow operation, like a database query
    data = {'message': 'This is cached data!'}
    return jsonify(data)

if __name__ == '__main__':
    app.run(debug=True)
```

In this example, the `@cache.cached()` decorator caches the response for the `/api/data` route for 60 seconds. This means that subsequent requests to the same endpoint within that timeframe will be served from the cache rather than recalculating or fetching the data again.

Benefits of Caching for Scalability:

- **Reduced Latency**: By serving data from the cache, response times are faster because accessing memory is much quicker than querying a database.
- **Offloading Database**: Caching reduces the number of database queries, which helps prevent database overload and improve performance under heavy traffic.

- **Improved Throughput**: With less load on the database, the overall throughput of your application increases.

In this chapter, we explored several essential strategies for building scalable APIs using Flask. We discussed **horizontal and vertical scaling**, including **sharding** and **replication** for optimizing database performance. We also delved into **real-time applications** with **Flask-SocketIO** for asynchronous communication and the importance of **caching** to improve scalability and reduce load. Finally, we examined various techniques to enhance performance and ensure that your Flask application can efficiently handle high traffic and large-scale operations. These strategies are key to building reliable, fast, and scalable APIs.

Chapter 8: Testing and Debugging Your API

8.1. Importance of Testing in API Development

Testing is a crucial part of the software development process, especially when building APIs. Without thorough testing, bugs and vulnerabilities can slip through, leading to unreliable performance and a poor user experience. In API development, the importance of testing cannot be overstated because APIs often act as the backbone of modern applications, connecting various services and handling sensitive data.

Why API Testing Matters:

1. **Ensures Functionality**: Testing ensures that your API behaves as expected. It verifies that your API correctly processes requests, returns the right responses, and integrates well with other services.
2. **Detects Bugs Early**: By writing tests for your API, you can catch bugs early in the development process, reducing the cost of fixing them later on.
3. **Improves API Reliability**: Automated tests help ensure that the API will continue to function as expected as you make changes or scale your application.
4. **Ensures Security**: Testing helps uncover security vulnerabilities such as SQL injections, unauthorized access, and data leaks, ensuring your API is secure and protects user data.
5. **Facilitates Refactoring and Maintenance**: When you need to refactor or extend your API, having tests in place ensures that the changes do not break existing functionality.

Types of Testing in API Development:

1. **Unit Testing**:
   - Focuses on testing individual components or functions of the API to ensure they work as intended in isolation.
   - Unit tests help verify the correctness of business logic, data transformations, and other small units of functionality.
2. **Integration Testing**:
   - Tests the interactions between components, such as the integration between your API and databases, external services, or other microservices.
   - Ensures that different parts of the system work together smoothly.
3. **End-to-End (E2E) Testing**:
   - Simulates real-world scenarios and tests the entire system from the user's perspective, ensuring the API meets business requirements.
   - Involves testing the full flow of an application, including the frontend and backend.
4. **Performance Testing**:
   - Ensures that the API performs well under load, with high traffic, or when performing resource-intensive tasks.
   - Involves testing response times, throughput, and error rates under various conditions.
5. **Security Testing**:
   - Focuses on identifying security vulnerabilities, such as SQL injection, cross-site scripting (XSS), and improper authorization.
   - Ensures the API is resistant to common attack vectors.

Testing is essential to ensuring that your API is robust, secure, and ready for production. In the following sections, we'll dive into how to write unit tests using **Pytest**, perform integration testing, and debug your Flask APIs.

8.2. Writing Unit Tests for Flask APIs with Pytest

Unit tests are essential to validate that individual pieces of your application's logic are working as expected. In Flask, unit testing is typically done using **Pytest**, a popular testing framework for Python that is simple, powerful, and easy to use.

Why Pytest?

Pytest is an excellent choice for testing Flask applications due to its simplicity, flexibility, and extensive ecosystem of plugins. It supports fixtures for setting up test data and has rich assertions to check the correctness of your application's behavior.

Setting Up Pytest with Flask

Install Pytest:
First, you need to install Pytest and the Flask testing utilities:
bash
Copy

```
pip install pytest pytest-flask
```

1. **Create a Test File**:
   Test files are typically stored in the `tests/` directory of your project, and test function names should start with `test_` for Pytest to recognize them. For example, let's create a file `test_app.py` to write our tests.

Test the Flask Application:
Below is a simple Flask app with a route that returns a JSON response:
python
Copy

```
from flask import Flask, jsonify
```

```python
app = Flask(__name__)

@app.route('/api/greet', methods=['GET'])
def greet():
    return jsonify(message="Hello, World!")

if __name__ == '__main__':
    app.run(debug=True)
```

2. **Write Unit Tests Using Pytest**:
   In the test_app.py file, we'll write unit tests for the /api/greet route to check that it returns the correct message.
   python
   Copy

```python
import pytest

from app import app  # Import the Flask app

@pytest.fixture
def client():
    # Create a test client for the Flask app
    with app.test_client() as client:
        yield client

def test_greet(client):
    """Test the /api/greet endpoint."""
    response = client.get('/api/greet')
    assert response.status_code == 200  # Check if status code is 200
    assert response.json == {'message': 'Hello, World!'}  # Check if the response is correct
```

3. In this example:
   - We use the @pytest.fixture decorator to create a client fixture that provides a test client for the Flask app.
   - The test_greet() function sends a **GET** request to the /api/greet route and verifies that the response's status code is 200 and the returned JSON matches the expected result.

Running the Tests:

To run the tests, execute the following command in the terminal:

bash

Copy

```
pytest
```

Pytest will automatically discover all test functions in your project (functions that start with test_) and execute them.

Best Practices for Unit Testing Flask APIs:

- **Isolate Tests**: Unit tests should test individual components in isolation without dependencies on external services (e.g., databases, third-party APIs).
- **Use Fixtures**: Pytest fixtures allow you to set up reusable test data, configurations, or state for your tests.
- **Mock External Services**: If your API depends on external services (e.g., a third-party API), use mocking libraries like unittest.mock or **pytest-mock** to simulate those services during testing.
- **Write Tests for Edge Cases**: Test for edge cases, invalid inputs, and unexpected behaviors to ensure your API handles these scenarios gracefully.

8.3. Integration Testing: Testing Endpoints and Databases

While unit testing ensures that individual functions or components work as expected, **integration testing** ensures that multiple components of your application interact correctly with each other. In the case of Flask APIs, integration testing typically focuses on testing the full API endpoints, including interaction with databases and other external services.

Why Integration Testing?

- **End-to-End Testing**: Integration tests check the flow of data through your API, ensuring that requests are properly processed and that the correct data is returned.
- **Database Interaction**: These tests ensure that the API correctly interacts with the database, performing actions such as creating, reading, updating, and deleting data (CRUD operations).

Setting Up Integration Tests for Flask APIs

To write integration tests for Flask APIs, we need to test how our routes interact with the database and ensure that the database state is updated correctly.

Set Up a Test Database:
It's important to use a separate test database to ensure that your production database remains unchanged during testing. You can configure a test-specific database URL in the Flask app's configuration.
Example of a test database configuration:
python
Copy

```
app.config['SQLALCHEMY_DATABASE_URI'] = 'sqlite:///test.db'  # Test database
app.config['SQLALCHEMY_TRACK_MODIFICATIONS'] = False
```

1. **Write Integration Tests**:

   Here's an example of how to test a Flask route that interacts with the database:

   python

   Copy

```
from flask import Flask, request, jsonify

from flask_sqlalchemy import SQLAlchemy
import pytest

app = Flask(__name__)
app.config['SQLALCHEMY_DATABASE_URI'] = 'sqlite:///test.db'
app.config['SQLALCHEMY_TRACK_MODIFICATIONS'] = False
db = SQLAlchemy(app)

# Define a simple User model
class User(db.Model):
    id = db.Column(db.Integer, primary_key=True)
    name = db.Column(db.String(100), nullable=False)

@app.route('/api/users', methods=['POST'])
def create_user():
    data = request.get_json()
    new_user = User(name=data['name'])
    db.session.add(new_user)
    db.session.commit()
    return jsonify({'id': new_user.id, 'name': new_user.name}), 201

# Write an integration test for the /api/users endpoint
@pytest.fixture
def client():
```

```
    db.create_all()  # Create tables for the test database
    with app.test_client() as client:
        yield client
    db.drop_all()  # Drop tables after tests are completed

def test_create_user(client):
    """Test creating a new user via the /api/users endpoint."""
    response = client.post('/api/users', json={'name': 'Alice'})
    assert response.status_code == 201
    assert response.json['name'] == 'Alice'
    assert 'id' in response.json
```

2. In this example:
    - The /api/users route creates a new user in the database when a **POST** request is made.
    - The test fixture client() sets up the test database and ensures that the database is cleaned up after the test.
    - The test_create_user() function sends a **POST** request to create a new user and verifies that the user is created correctly in the database.

Running Integration Tests:

As with unit tests, you can run integration tests using Pytest:

bash

Copy

```
pytest
```

3. **Best Practices for Integration Testing:**

- **Isolate the Database**: Use a separate test database to avoid modifying production data.

- **Clean Up After Tests**: Ensure that your tests clean up by rolling back transactions or deleting test data after they run.
- **Test All API Routes**: Write integration tests for all your API endpoints, covering common use cases and edge cases.
- **Test Database Integrity**: Ensure that changes to the database are correctly persisted (e.g., data is saved, updated, or deleted as expected).

We discussed the importance of **testing** and **debugging** your Flask API. We explored how to write **unit tests** using **Pytest** to ensure that individual components function as expected and how to perform **integration testing** to test the interactions between your API and the database. By testing thoroughly, you ensure that your API remains reliable, secure, and efficient as you make changes and scale your application. With these practices in place, you can confidently develop and deploy Flask APIs with strong test coverage.

8.4. Using Flask-Testing for Test Automation

Testing your Flask APIs is an essential practice to ensure reliability, but automating the tests can significantly improve the efficiency of your development process. **Flask-Testing** is an extension that makes testing Flask applications easier by providing utilities and helpers specifically designed for Flask apps. It simplifies the process of writing tests and automating test execution.

What is Flask-Testing?

Flask-Testing provides a set of tools to facilitate unit tests and functional tests for Flask applications. It offers helpful features like:

- Test case classes to simplify the testing of Flask applications.
- Built-in support for handling Flask's app and client.

- Helper functions to interact with Flask's test client and test configurations.

Setting Up Flask-Testing

Install Flask-Testing:

To use Flask-Testing, you need to install it via pip:

bash

Copy

```
pip install Flask-Testing
```

1. **Integrating Flask-Testing**:

   After installing, you can use it to write your tests. Here's a basic setup for using Flask-Testing with your Flask app.

   python

   Copy

```
from flask import Flask, jsonify

from flask_testing import TestCase


app = Flask(__name__)


@app.route('/api/greet', methods=['GET'])
def greet():
    return jsonify(message="Hello, World!")


class MyTestCase(TestCase):
    def create_app(self):
        app.config['TESTING'] = True
        return app


    def test_greet(self):
```

```
    """Test the /api/greet endpoint"""
    response = self.client.get('/api/greet')
    self.assertEqual(response.status_code, 200)
    self.assertEqual(response.json, {'message': 'Hello, World!'})

if __name__ == '__main__':
  app.run(debug=True)
```

2. In this example:
   - We define a route /api/greet that returns a greeting.
   - The MyTestCase class inherits from flask_testing.TestCase, and the create_app method is overridden to configure the Flask app for testing.
   - The test_greet method tests that the /api/greet endpoint returns the expected status code and JSON data.

Running the Tests:

Once your tests are written using Flask-Testing, you can run them just like with Pytest:

bash

Copy

```
pytest
```

Flask-Testing integrates with Pytest, so you can continue using your test runner of choice. Flask-Testing also provides useful methods like assertEqual(), assertIn(), and others, making assertions in your tests simple and readable.

Benefits of Using Flask-Testing:

- **Simplifies Setup**: The TestCase class takes care of setting up and tearing down the Flask app for each test, reducing boilerplate code.

- **Improved Assertions**: Flask-Testing offers enhanced assertion methods tailored for Flask applications, improving test readability and maintainability.
- **Configuration Management**: Flask-Testing allows you to manage test-specific configuration easily, ensuring your app runs in a safe, isolated environment during tests.

8.5. Debugging Common API Errors

Debugging is an essential part of the development process, especially when working with Flask APIs. As your application grows and you introduce new features or make changes, errors can surface. Identifying and fixing errors quickly can help keep your API reliable and performant.

Common API Errors in Flask

1. **404 Not Found**: This error occurs when the client tries to access a route that doesn't exist or isn't registered correctly.
   - **Solution**: Check the route definitions in your Flask app. Make sure that the endpoint is correctly mapped and that the URL is accurate.
   - **Example**: If you have a typo in the route path or if the method (GET, POST, etc.) does not match, Flask will return a 404 error.

python

Copy

```
@app.route('/api/user', methods=['GET'])
def get_user():
    return jsonify({"user": "Alice"})
```

2. If you try to access /api/userr instead of /api/user, it will return a 404 error.

3. **500 Internal Server Error**: This is a general error indicating that something went wrong on the server side. It could be caused by various issues like bugs in the code, database errors, or invalid data processing.
   - **Solution**: Check the server logs for more detailed error messages. Flask's debug mode (app.debug = True) can also provide stack traces to help identify the issue.
   - **Example**: If you are querying the database and the database connection fails, Flask will throw a 500 error.
4. **400 Bad Request**: This error occurs when the client sends invalid data, such as missing required fields or improperly formatted requests.
   - **Solution**: Check that the request body, headers, and query parameters match what the API expects. For example, ensure that the client sends the correct JSON format for POST requests.

python

Copy

```python
@app.route('/api/create', methods=['POST'])
def create_resource():
    if not request.json or 'name' not in request.json:
        return jsonify({'error': 'Missing name field'}), 400
    # Continue processing if request is valid
```

5. If the client doesn't include the name field in the JSON body, it will return a 400 Bad Request error.
6. **405 Method Not Allowed**: This error occurs when the client sends a request using an HTTP method that is not allowed for a specific route (e.g., a POST request to a route that only allows GET).
   - **Solution**: Check the allowed methods for your routes and make sure the client is using the correct HTTP method.

python

Copy

```
@app.route('/api/update', methods=['PUT'])
def update_resource():
    # Allow only PUT method
    return jsonify({"message": "Updated successfully"})
```

7. **400 Unauthorized (Authentication Errors)**: This error happens when the client attempts to access a protected route without valid authentication credentials (e.g., a missing or invalid token).
   - **Solution**: Implement proper authentication mechanisms (such as JWT tokens) and ensure that clients are sending the correct headers or tokens with requests.

python

Copy

```
@app.route('/api/protected', methods=['GET'])
@auth.login_required
def protected_route():
    return jsonify({"message": "Access granted"})
```

Flask Debugging Tools

1. **Flask Debug Mode**:
   - Flask's debug mode provides detailed error messages and stack traces when errors occur, which helps with quick identification of issues.
   - To enable debug mode, set `app.debug = True` or use `app.run(debug=True)` when running the app.

2. **Flask Logging**:
   - You can log errors and other useful information using Python's logging module. Flask allows you to configure logging to display or record detailed error messages for debugging purposes.

Example:

python

Copy

```
import logging

app = Flask(__name__)
app.logger.setLevel(logging.DEBUG)  # Set log level to DEBUG for detailed logs

@app.route('/api/debug', methods=['GET'])
def debug_route():
    app.logger.debug('Debug message')
    return jsonify({"message": "Check the logs"})
```

3. **Use a Debugger**:
   - Python debuggers like **pdb** or **IPython** can be integrated with Flask to inspect variables and step through code interactively.

Example:

python

Copy

```
import pdb

@app.route('/api/test', methods=['GET'])
def test_route():
    pdb.set_trace()  # Set a breakpoint here
    return jsonify({"message": "Testing breakpoint"})
```

4. This will pause execution at the pdb.set_trace() line, allowing you to interactively debug your Flask application.

8.6. Test-Driven Development (TDD) for Flask APIs

Test-Driven Development (TDD) is a software development approach where tests are written before writing the actual code. TDD helps ensure that your API works as expected and encourages writing minimal, clean code to pass the tests.

Benefits of TDD:

- **Improved Code Quality**: Writing tests first encourages developers to write code that is easy to test and maintain.
- **Faster Debugging**: By writing tests upfront, you catch bugs early in the development process.
- **Better Documentation**: The tests serve as documentation for how your API should behave, making it easier for other developers to understand the system.

Writing Tests First in Flask

Start with Test Cases: Begin by writing the tests for your Flask API endpoints and business logic. For example, if you want to create an endpoint for user registration, you would write a test first.

python

Copy

```
def test_register_user(client):
    response = client.post('/api/register', json={'name': 'John', 'email':
'john@example.com'})
    assert response.status_code == 201
    assert response.json['message'] == 'User created'
```

1. **Implement the Code**: After writing the test, implement the functionality to make the test pass. In this case, you would write the code for the /api/register route to handle user creation.
   python
   Copy

```python
@app.route('/api/register', methods=['POST'])

def register_user():
    data = request.get_json()
    if not data.get('name') or not data.get('email'):
        return jsonify({'error': 'Missing fields'}), 400
    return jsonify({'message': 'User created'}), 201
```

2. **Refactor and Repeat**: Once the test passes, you can refactor the code and add more tests as needed. Refactoring should not break the existing tests.

Example of a TDD Cycle:

1. **Red**: Write a failing test.
2. **Green**: Write the minimal code to pass the test.
3. **Refactor**: Refactor the code to improve readability and performance while ensuring the tests continue to pass.

TDD is an iterative process where tests and code are developed together. By using TDD, you can ensure your API is well-tested, reliable, and maintainable.

We discussed the importance of testing and debugging your Flask APIs. We explored **Flask-Testing** for automating tests, techniques for **debugging common API errors**, and how to implement **Test-Driven Development (TDD)** for Flask APIs. Testing and debugging are essential practices for building reliable, scalable, and maintainable APIs, and using tools like **Pytest**, **Flask-Testing**, and **TDD** can significantly improve the development process. By incorporating these practices into your workflow, you ensure that your API is robust, secure, and performs as expected under various conditions.

Chapter 9: Dockerizing Flask APIs

9.1. Introduction to Docker and Its Benefits for API Development

In the world of modern web development, **Docker** has become an essential tool for packaging, deploying, and running applications. Docker is a platform that enables you to develop, ship, and run applications in lightweight, portable containers. These containers encapsulate all the necessary dependencies, configurations, and environments, ensuring that your application runs consistently across different systems.

What is Docker?

Docker is a containerization platform that packages an application and its dependencies into a standardized unit known as a **container**. A container is a lightweight, executable package that includes everything needed to run the application—such as the code, runtime, libraries, environment variables, and system tools.

Containers are isolated from the host system and each other, providing a consistent environment that eliminates the "it works on my machine" problem. Docker uses a simple and efficient architecture where you define your environment using **Dockerfiles**, and then Docker can automatically build, ship, and run your application.

Benefits of Docker for API Development:

1. **Consistency Across Environments**:
    - With Docker, you can ensure that your API will work on any system (local development, staging, production) as it runs inside the same container regardless of the underlying host OS. This eliminates issues caused by environment inconsistencies.

2. **Isolation**:
    - Docker containers isolate applications, which means they won't interfere with each other. For example, you can run multiple Flask applications on the same host without conflicts between dependencies.
3. **Scalability**:
    - Docker enables horizontal scaling by allowing you to quickly spin up additional containers for increased traffic. It works seamlessly with orchestration tools like **Kubernetes** to manage multiple containers.
4. **Faster Development Cycle**:
    - Docker reduces the time it takes to set up environments and dependencies, making the development cycle faster. It allows you to run your application without worrying about system-specific issues.
5. **Simplified Deployment**:
    - With Docker, you can package your application, including all its dependencies, into a single container. This simplifies the deployment process, as you only need to worry about running the container rather than configuring the environment on each server.
6. **Versioning and Reproducibility**:
    - Docker allows you to version containers and reproduce environments consistently, which is particularly useful in both development and production.

Docker for Flask APIs:

Docker provides an excellent way to package Flask applications, making them easier to deploy and scale. It also allows developers to create a repeatable, consistent environment for running APIs, regardless of the host machine's configuration. This section will guide you through creating and managing Docker containers for Flask APIs.

9.2. Creating a Dockerfile for Your Flask API

A **Dockerfile** is a text document that contains instructions on how to build a Docker image. The Docker image is essentially a blueprint for creating Docker containers. For Flask API development, the Dockerfile defines how to set up the environment, install dependencies, and run the application inside a container.

Steps to Create a Dockerfile for a Flask API:

Let's walk through the steps to create a simple Dockerfile for a Flask application.

Start with the Base Image:
You need to specify a base image that provides the operating system and environment your application needs. For Flask, a good choice is the official **Python image** from Docker Hub.

Dockerfile

Copy

```
FROM python:3.8-slim
```

1. The `python:3.8-slim` image is a lightweight version of the official Python image and includes only the necessary components to run Python.

Set the Working Directory:
You should set a working directory inside the container where your application's code will live. This is typically done using the `WORKDIR` command.

Dockerfile

Copy

```
WORKDIR /app
```

2. **Copy the Application Code**:

   Next, you'll copy the Flask application code into the container. The COPY command copies files from your local machine into the container.

   Dockerfile

   Copy

   ```
   COPY . /app
   ```

3. This will copy all the files in your project directory to the /app directory inside the container.

Install Dependencies:

It's common practice to define your dependencies in a requirements.txt file. This file lists all the Python packages your Flask app needs. You can install these dependencies using the RUN command.

Dockerfile

Copy

```
RUN pip install --no-cache-dir -r requirements.txt
```

4. This will install the dependencies into the container. The --no-cache-dir option ensures that pip doesn't cache the downloaded packages, reducing the image size.

Expose the Port:

Flask typically runs on port 5000. You need to tell Docker to expose this port to make the application accessible.

Dockerfile

Copy

```
EXPOSE 5000
```

5. **Run the Flask Application**:

   Finally, you need to tell Docker how to run the Flask app inside the container. This is done with the CMD command, which specifies the command to run when the container starts.

   Dockerfile

   Copy

   ```
   CMD ["flask", "run", "--host=0.0.0.0"]
   ```

6. The --host=0.0.0.0 flag tells Flask to listen on all available network interfaces, making the app accessible outside the container.

Complete Dockerfile Example:

Dockerfile

Copy

```
# Use a lightweight Python image as a base
FROM python:3.8-slim

# Set the working directory inside the container
WORKDIR /app

# Copy the application files into the container
COPY . /app

# Install dependencies
RUN pip install --no-cache-dir -r requirements.txt

# Expose the port that the Flask app will run on
EXPOSE 5000

# Run the Flask application
```

```
CMD ["flask", "run", "--host=0.0.0.0"]
```

9.3. Managing Docker Containers: Building, Running, and Testing

Once the Dockerfile is ready, you can proceed with building the Docker image and running your Flask application inside a container. This section will walk you through the process of building, running, and testing your Dockerized Flask API.

Step 1: Building the Docker Image

To build a Docker image, you use the `docker build` command. Make sure you are in the directory where your `Dockerfile` is located.

bash

Copy

```
docker build -t flask-api .
```

- `-t flask-api` tags the image with the name `flask-api`.
- `.` indicates the current directory as the build context.

This command reads the `Dockerfile`, installs the dependencies, and creates an image with the Flask app.

Step 2: Running the Docker Container

Once the image is built, you can run it using the `docker run` command. This will start a container from the image and map port 5000 on the container to port 5000 on your host machine.

bash

Copy

```
docker run -p 5000:5000 flask-api
```

- -p 5000:5000 maps port 5000 on the container to port 5000 on your host machine. Now, your Flask app will be accessible at http://localhost:5000.

If everything is set up correctly, you should see Flask start running in the terminal, and you can visit http://localhost:5000 to interact with your API.

Step 3: Testing the Dockerized Flask API

To test your Dockerized Flask application, you can use tools like **curl**, **Postman**, or **pytest** to send requests to the running container.

For example, using curl to test a route:

bash

Copy

```
curl http://localhost:5000/api/greet
```

If the API is working, you should get a response with the expected JSON data.

Step 4: Stopping the Docker Container

When you are done testing or running the container, you can stop it by pressing Ctrl+C in the terminal or by using the docker stop command:

bash

Copy

```
docker ps  # Get the container ID
docker stop <container_id>  # Stop the container
```

Step 5: Managing Docker Containers

- **List Running Containers**: To list all running containers, use `docker ps`.
- **View Container Logs**: To view logs from a running container, use `docker logs <container_id>`.
- **Remove Stopped Containers**: You can remove a container once it's stopped by using `docker rm <container_id>`.
- **Clean Up Images**: You can remove unused images with `docker rmi <image_id>` to free up space.

We introduced **Docker** and discussed its benefits for API development. Dockerizing your Flask API ensures consistent environments, portability, and easy deployment across different systems. We walked through the process of creating a **Dockerfile** to define the environment and building, running, and testing Docker containers for Flask applications. Dockerization simplifies deployment, scaling, and management of Flask APIs, making it an essential tool for modern application development.

9.4. Multi-Stage Builds for Production-Ready Flask Applications

When Dockerizing a Flask application, it's common to use a **multi-stage build** to create a production-ready image. A multi-stage build allows you to optimize your Docker images by separating the build and runtime environments. This approach helps reduce the size of your final image, improves security, and ensures that only the necessary files are included in your production container.

What is a Multi-Stage Build?

In a **multi-stage build**, Docker allows you to define multiple FROM instructions in the same Dockerfile. Each FROM represents a new build stage. This technique enables you to build your application in one stage and copy only the necessary artifacts (such as compiled code, dependencies, and configuration files) to the final, smaller runtime image.

Benefits of Multi-Stage Builds:

1. **Smaller Image Size**: By using separate stages, you can avoid including unnecessary build dependencies (such as compilers and source code) in the final image, making it smaller and more efficient.
2. **Improved Security**: By leaving build tools and dependencies behind, you reduce the attack surface of the production container.
3. **Cleaner Production Environment**: The final image contains only what is needed to run the application, not the tools used to build it.

Example of a Multi-Stage Dockerfile for Flask

Let's take a look at a multi-stage Dockerfile for a Flask API. The first stage is for building the application, and the second stage is for running it in production.

Dockerfile

Copy

```
# Build Stage: Use a Python image with all build dependencies
FROM python:3.8-slim as builder

# Set the working directory inside the container
WORKDIR /app

# Copy the application code and install dependencies
```

```
COPY . /app
RUN pip install --no-cache-dir -r requirements.txt

# Production Stage: Use a smaller Python image for running the app
FROM python:3.8-slim as production

# Set the working directory in the production container
WORKDIR /app

# Copy only the necessary files from the builder stage
COPY --from=builder /app /app

# Expose the application port
EXPOSE 5000

# Set environment variable for Flask app
ENV FLASK_APP=app.py

# Run the Flask application
CMD ["flask", "run", "--host=0.0.0.0"]
```

Explanation of the Dockerfile:

1. **Build Stage**:
   - The first stage uses python:3.8-slim as the base image and sets up the build environment.
   - The application code is copied, and dependencies are installed via pip.
2. **Production Stage**:

    - The second stage uses the same python:3.8-slim image (without the build dependencies) to create the final runtime environment.
    - The necessary application files (installed dependencies, code) are copied from the builder stage into the production image.
3. **Exposing Port and Running the App**:
    - The final container exposes port 5000 and runs the Flask application using the flask run command.

Benefits of this Multi-Stage Build:

- **Smaller Image Size**: The final image only contains the Python runtime, your app, and its dependencies, not the build tools.
- **Cleaner Environment**: It eliminates unnecessary files and build tools from the final production image, leading to a cleaner and more secure container.

9.5. Using Docker Compose for Complex Applications

For more complex applications that involve multiple services (e.g., a Flask app, a database, caching system, or a message queue), **Docker Compose** is a powerful tool that simplifies the management of multi-container Docker applications. Docker Compose allows you to define and manage all the services in a single configuration file (docker-compose.yml), making it easier to manage dependencies and configurations.

What is Docker Compose?

Docker Compose is a tool for defining and running multi-container Docker applications. With Compose, you can define all of your app's services, networks, and volumes in a single YAML file, and then run everything with a single command.

Example: Docker Compose for Flask, PostgreSQL, and Redis

Let's assume you have a Flask API that interacts with a PostgreSQL database and uses Redis for caching. Here's how you could define the services using Docker Compose:

1. **Create the docker-compose.yml File**:

yaml

Copy

```
version: '3'
services:
  flask:
    build: .
    container_name: flask-api
    ports:
      - "5000:5000"
    environment:
      - FLASK_ENV=development
      - FLASK_APP=app.py
    depends_on:
      - postgres
      - redis

  postgres:
    image: postgres:13
    container_name: postgres-db
    environment:
      POSTGRES_USER: user
      POSTGRES_PASSWORD: password
      POSTGRES_DB: flaskdb
```

```
    volumes:
      - postgres_data:/var/lib/postgresql/data
    ports:
      - "5432:5432"

  redis:
    image: redis:alpine
    container_name: redis-cache
    ports:
      - "6379:6379"

volumes:
  postgres_data:
```

Explanation of the docker-compose.yml file:

1. **Flask Service**:
    - This service is built using the Dockerfile in the current directory (denoted by .).
    - The Flask application is mapped to port 5000 and is set to run in development mode with the FLASK_ENV=development environment variable.
    - The Flask app depends on the postgres and redis services, meaning they must be started first.
2. **PostgreSQL Service**:
    - This service uses the official PostgreSQL image and sets up a database named flaskdb with a user and password.
    - The postgres_data volume ensures that the database data is persistent across container restarts.

3. **Redis Service**:
   - This service uses the official Redis image to set up a Redis server for caching purposes.
4. **Volumes**:
   - The postgres_data volume is defined to persist PostgreSQL data even when the container is stopped or recreated.

Step 1: Build and Start the Containers:

Once your docker-compose.yml file is ready, you can use the following command to build and start the containers:

bash

Copy

```
docker-compose up --build
```

- This command builds the images (if they haven't been built already) and starts the services defined in the docker-compose.yml file.

Step 2: Accessing the Application:

After the services are running, your Flask app should be accessible at http://localhost:5000. You can interact with the PostgreSQL database and Redis cache through your Flask application, and Docker Compose handles managing the containers and networking between them.

Step 3: Stopping the Containers:

You can stop the running containers using:

bash

Copy

```
docker-compose down
```

This stops the services and removes the containers. If you want to stop the services without removing the containers, use `docker-compose stop`.

9.6. Best Practices for Dockerizing Flask APIs

When Dockerizing Flask APIs, it's important to follow best practices to ensure that your containers are secure, efficient, and easy to maintain. Here are some essential tips for optimizing Docker containers for Flask applications:

1. Minimize the Image Size

- Use **multi-stage builds** to reduce the size of your final image by separating the build and runtime stages.
- Choose a **lightweight base image** like `python:3.8-slim` instead of a larger one like `python:3.8` to keep your image lean.
- Avoid installing unnecessary dependencies or build tools that are only required during the build stage.

2. Environment Variables for Configuration

- Use **environment variables** for configuring your Flask app (e.g., database credentials, secret keys, environment-specific settings). This makes your application more flexible and secure.
- You can pass environment variables in the `docker-compose.yml` file or in the `Dockerfile` using the `ENV` command.

3. Use Volumes for Persistent Data

- Use **Docker volumes** to persist data between container restarts. This is particularly important for databases (e.g., PostgreSQL, MongoDB) and other services that require persistent data storage.
- For example, use volumes to store the PostgreSQL database data or Redis cache so that data is not lost when the container is stopped or recreated.

4. Avoid Running Flask in Debug Mode in Production

- While Flask's debug mode is useful during development, it should never be enabled in production. Debug mode can expose sensitive information and make your application more vulnerable to attacks.
- Set the environment variable `FLASK_ENV=production` or set `app.config['ENV'] = 'production'` to ensure that debug mode is disabled.

5. Optimize Network Configurations

- By default, Docker containers communicate with each other over a private network. Ensure that you use Docker's **networking** features to isolate and secure communication between services.
- Use **Docker Compose** to define services and manage the networking between them in a structured and organized manner.

6. Keep Docker Images Updated

- Regularly update your Docker images, especially the base images, to ensure that they include the latest security patches and updates.
- Use the latest stable versions of libraries and tools to ensure that your Flask API remains secure.

7. Health Checks for Production

Use **Docker health checks** to automatically monitor and restart your Flask application if it becomes unresponsive or crashes. You can add a health check to your docker-compose.yml or Dockerfile:

Dockerfile

Copy

```
HEALTHCHECK CMD curl --fail http://localhost:5000/health || exit 1
```

- This will automatically check if the Flask app is running correctly and restart the container if needed.

In this chapter, we covered the essential steps for **Dockerizing Flask APIs**. We explored **multi-stage builds** to optimize image size for production, discussed using **Docker Compose** for handling complex applications with multiple services, and provided best practices to ensure your Flask API containers are efficient, secure, and scalable. Docker makes it easy to containerize your Flask API, simplifying deployment, scalability, and maintenance. By following these best practices, you can ensure that your application is production-ready and optimized for high performance.

Chapter 10: Deploying Your API

10.1. Preparing Your Flask API for Production

Before deploying your Flask API to production, there are several steps you need to follow to ensure that your application runs efficiently, securely, and is ready to handle real-world traffic. Deploying directly from a development environment to production without any preparation can lead to performance issues, security vulnerabilities, and downtime.

Key Steps for Preparing Flask for Production:

1. **Disable Debug Mode**:
   - In development, Flask's debug mode provides useful error messages and automatic reloading. However, it should be disabled in production to avoid exposing sensitive information and to improve performance.

In production, ensure that the following settings are configured:

python

Copy

```
app.config['DEBUG'] = False
app.config['ENV'] = 'production'
```

2. **Set the Flask Secret Key**:

Flask uses a secret key for signing cookies and sessions. You should configure a strong, random secret key for production. Do not hardcode the secret key in your code; instead, use an environment variable to securely store it.

python

Copy

```
import os
app.config['SECRET_KEY'] = os.getenv('FLASK_SECRET_KEY',
'default_secret_key')
```

3. **Use a Production-Ready WSGI Server**:
   - Flask's built-in development server (`flask run`) is not suitable for production. It's single-threaded and lacks performance optimizations. In production, you should use a **WSGI server** like **Gunicorn** or **uWSGI**.

Install **Gunicorn**:

bash

Copy

```
pip install gunicorn
```

Run the application using Gunicorn:

bash

Copy

```
gunicorn app:app --bind 0.0.0.0:5000
```

4. **Configure Database Connections**:
   - In production, databases often use connection pooling to optimize resource usage. Configure your database connection to use proper connection pooling settings. Additionally, use a separate production database rather than using the local development one.

Example for SQLAlchemy with PostgreSQL:

python

Copy

```
app.config['SQLALCHEMY_DATABASE_URI'] = os.getenv('DATABASE_URL')
app.config['SQLALCHEMY_POOL_SIZE'] = 10  # Example of connection pooling
```

5. **Implement Logging**:

Production applications should have proper logging to track errors and monitor performance. Flask can log errors and events using the built-in logging module. Ensure that logs are written to files or external services (e.g., AWS CloudWatch, Papertrail) for monitoring.

Example:

python

Copy

```
import logging
from logging.handlers import RotatingFileHandler

handler = RotatingFileHandler('app.log', maxBytes=10000, backupCount=3)
handler.setLevel(logging.INFO)
app.logger.addHandler(handler)
```

6. **Optimize Static Files**:
   - In production, static files (CSS, JavaScript, images) should be served efficiently. You can use a reverse proxy like **NGINX** or a CDN to serve static content. Flask has built-in support for static files, but it's more efficient to offload this to a dedicated web server.
7. **Security Best Practices**:
   - **Use HTTPS**: Use **SSL/TLS** certificates to encrypt communication. This is essential for protecting sensitive data, especially in public-facing APIs.
   - **Rate Limiting**: Protect your API from abuse by implementing rate limiting to prevent excessive requests from the same client.
   - **Cross-Origin Resource Sharing (CORS)**: Use Flask-CORS to control which domains are allowed to make requests to your API.

10.2. Deploying to Heroku: A Simple Approach for Beginners

Heroku is one of the easiest platforms for beginners to deploy web applications, including Flask APIs. It abstracts away much of the complexity involved in deployment, providing a platform-as-a-service (PaaS) that automatically handles infrastructure, scaling, and monitoring.

Steps for Deploying Flask API to Heroku:

1. **Set Up Heroku Account**:
    1. Sign up for a free Heroku account at heroku.com.

Install the **Heroku CLI** to manage your Heroku applications from the command line.

bash

Copy

```
curl https://cli-assets.heroku.com/install.sh | sh
```

2. **Prepare the Flask App for Deployment**:
    1. Make sure you have the following files in your project:
        - Procfile: This file tells Heroku how to run your Flask app.
        - requirements.txt: This file lists all the dependencies for your Flask app.
        - runtime.txt: Optional, but it specifies the version of Python to use.

Procfile:

plaintext

Copy

```
web: gunicorn app:app
```

This tells Heroku to run the Flask app using Gunicorn.

requirements.txt:

Generate a requirements.txt file that lists all the dependencies of your app.

bash

Copy

```
pip freeze > requirements.txt
```

runtime.txt:

Specify the Python version you want to use (optional):

plaintext

Copy

```
python-3.8.10
```

3. **Create and Deploy the Application**:

Initialize a Git repository if you haven't already:

bash

Copy

```
git init
git add .
git commit -m "Initial commit"
```

1. **Login to Heroku** using the CLI:

   bash

   Copy

   ```
   heroku login
   ```

2. **Create a Heroku app**:

   bash

   Copy

   ```
   heroku create flask-api-app
   ```

3. This will create a new app and set a remote called `heroku` in your Git repository.

Deploy your app:

bash

Copy

```
git push heroku master
```

4. Heroku will automatically detect that your app is a Python application, install the dependencies, and start the app using Gunicorn.

4. **Access Your Flask API**:
   Once the deployment is complete, you can access your Flask app by navigating to the URL provided by Heroku (e.g., https://flask-api-app.herokuapp.com).

Setting Environment Variables:

To set environment variables like your database URL or secret key, you can use the Heroku CLI:

bash

Copy

```
heroku config:set FLASK_SECRET_KEY=your_secret_key
heroku config:set DATABASE_URL=your_database_url
```

5. **Scaling the Application**:
   To scale your application, such as increasing the number of web dynos (containers), use the following command:
   bash
   Copy
   ```
   heroku ps:scale web=1
   ```

10.3. Using AWS EC2 for Scalable API Deployment

For more advanced, scalable deployments, **AWS EC2** (Elastic Compute Cloud) provides a flexible infrastructure for hosting Flask APIs. EC2 instances are virtual servers where you can run your application, and AWS provides numerous services like **Auto Scaling** and **Load Balancing** to ensure your application can handle varying levels of traffic.

Steps for Deploying Flask API on AWS EC2:

1. **Create an AWS Account**:
   - Sign up for an AWS account at aws.amazon.com.
   - Log into the **AWS Management Console**.
2. **Launch an EC2 Instance**:
   - Go to the **EC2 Dashboard** and click on **Launch Instance**.
   - Select an **Amazon Linux 2** or **Ubuntu** AMI (Amazon Machine Image).
   - Choose an instance type (e.g., **t2.micro** for small-scale applications).
   - Configure instance details, such as VPC (Virtual Private Cloud), storage, and tags.
   - Add a **Security Group** with rules allowing inbound HTTP (port 80) and SSH (port 22) access.
   - Launch the instance and download the private key file (.pem) to connect via SSH.

Connect to the EC2 Instance:

Once the EC2 instance is running, connect to it using SSH. For example:

bash

Copy

```
ssh -i "your-key.pem" ec2-user@your-ec2-public-ip
```

3. **Install Dependencies on EC2**:

   Update the package index and install Python, Git, and other dependencies:

   bash

   Copy

```
sudo yum update -y  # For Amazon Linux
sudo yum install python3 git -y
```

4. If using Ubuntu, replace yum with apt for installation.

Clone Your Flask API Repository:

Clone your Flask app repository from GitHub (or use scp to copy your app directly to EC2):

bash

Copy

```
git clone https://github.com/yourusername/flask-api.git
cd flask-api
```

5. **Set Up Virtual Environment**:

   Set up a virtual environment on the EC2 instance:

   bash

   Copy

```
python3 -m venv venv
source venv/bin/activate
```

6. **Install Application Dependencies**:

   Install the dependencies from requirements.txt:

   bash

   Copy

```
pip install -r requirements.txt
```

7. **Install and Run Gunicorn**:

   Install **Gunicorn** (a production WSGI server) and run the Flask app:

   bash

   Copy

```
pip install gunicorn

gunicorn app:app --bind 0.0.0.0:80
```

8. This starts your Flask API on port 80 (the standard HTTP port).

Configure NGINX as a Reverse Proxy:

To route traffic to your Flask application, set up **NGINX** as a reverse proxy:

bash

Copy

```
sudo yum install nginx -y
sudo service nginx start
```

Configure NGINX to forward requests to your Flask application by editing the NGINX configuration file:

bash

Copy

```
sudo nano /etc/nginx/nginx.conf
```

Add the following inside the `server` block:

nginx

Copy

```
location / {
    proxy_pass http://localhost:5000;
    proxy_set_header Host $host;
    proxy_set_header X-Real-IP $remote_addr;
    proxy_set_header X-Forwarded-For $proxy_add_x_forwarded_for;
}
```

Restart NGINX:

bash

Copy

```
sudo service nginx restart
```

9. **Access Your Flask API**:
   Now you can access your Flask API by navigating to the EC2 instance's public IP in a web browser.

We covered the key steps for deploying your Flask API to production. First, we discussed how to **prepare** your Flask app for production, including disabling debug mode and using a production-ready WSGI server like Gunicorn. We then explored how to deploy a Flask API to **Heroku**, which is perfect for beginners, and how to use **AWS EC2** for more scalable and flexible deployment. By following these steps, you can deploy your Flask API with confidence and ensure it's ready for real-world traffic and use cases.

10.4. Setting Up Continuous Integration and Continuous Deployment (CI/CD)

Continuous Integration (CI) and Continuous Deployment (CD) are essential practices for modern software development. CI/CD pipelines automate the process of testing, building, and deploying your Flask API, allowing you to deliver updates and fixes quickly and reliably.

What is Continuous Integration (CI)?

Continuous Integration involves automatically running tests and building your Flask application whenever code is committed to the repository. CI ensures that the codebase remains in a deployable state at all times by verifying the functionality of the app through automated tests.

What is Continuous Deployment (CD)?

Continuous Deployment extends CI by automatically deploying your application to production after it passes the CI checks. This practice reduces manual intervention and allows new features and bug fixes to reach production quickly and reliably.

Setting Up CI/CD for Flask API Using GitHub Actions

GitHub Actions is a popular tool for setting up CI/CD pipelines directly from your GitHub repository. Here's how you can set up a simple CI/CD pipeline for your Flask API.

1. Create a `.github/workflows` Directory

In your repository, create the following directory structure:

bash

Copy

```
mkdir -p .github/workflows
```

2. Create a CI Workflow File

Inside the `.github/workflows` directory, create a file called `ci.yml` for setting up CI:

yaml

Copy

```yaml
name: Flask CI Workflow

on:
  push:
    branches:
      - main  # Trigger workflow on push to the main branch
  pull_request:
    branches:
      - main  # Trigger workflow on pull requests to the main branch

jobs:
  build:
    runs-on: ubuntu-latest

    steps:
    - name: Checkout Code
      uses: actions/checkout@v2

    - name: Set up Python
```

```
      uses: actions/setup-python@v2
      with:
        python-version: '3.8'  # Specify Python version

    - name: Install dependencies
      run: |
        python -m pip install --upgrade pip
        pip install -r requirements.txt

    - name: Run Tests
      run: |
        pytest  # Run tests using pytest
```

This workflow will:

- Trigger when code is pushed to the main branch or a pull request is made.
- Install Python dependencies.
- Run tests using **pytest**.

3. Create a CD Workflow File

Now, let's set up the **Continuous Deployment** workflow using a separate file called cd.yml in the .github/workflows directory:

yaml

Copy

```yaml
name: Flask CD Workflow

on:
  push:
    branches:
      - main  # Deploy when code is pushed to the main branch

jobs:
  deploy:
    runs-on: ubuntu-latest

    steps:
    - name: Checkout Code
      uses: actions/checkout@v2

    - name: Deploy to Heroku
      uses: akshaybabloo/heroku-deploy@v1.0.1
```


•

```
with:
  heroku_email: ${{ secrets.HEROKU_EMAIL }}
  heroku_api_key: ${{ secrets.HEROKU_API_KEY }}
  heroku_app_name: flask-api-app
```

This workflow will:

- Deploy the Flask app to Heroku whenever a push is made to the `main` branch.
- The `HEROKU_EMAIL` and `HEROKU_API_KEY` are stored as GitHub secrets for security.

4. Set Up GitHub Secrets

To keep your Heroku API key and email secure, you should store them in GitHub Secrets:

1. Go to your GitHub repository.
2. Click on **Settings** > **Secrets**.
3. Add `HEROKU_EMAIL` and `HEROKU_API_KEY` as secrets.

5. Running the CI/CD Pipeline

Once you've set up these workflows, GitHub Actions will automatically run the CI workflow when you push changes to the `main` branch or create a pull request. If the tests pass, the CD workflow will deploy your application to Heroku.

10.5. Monitoring Flask APIs in Production

Once your Flask API is deployed to production, it's crucial to monitor its performance, uptime, and overall health. Monitoring helps you track any issues and ensure that your API provides a reliable service.

Key Metrics to Monitor:

1. **Response Time**: Track the time it takes for your API to respond to requests. Long response times can indicate performance bottlenecks.
2. **Request Rate**: Monitor the number of incoming requests to your API. An unexpected increase in request rate may suggest a sudden spike in traffic or potential issues.
3. **Error Rate**: Monitor how often errors (e.g., HTTP 500 or 404 responses) occur. A high error rate can indicate problems with your application.
4. **Uptime**: Track the availability of your API. Downtime can impact user experience and business operations.
5. **Resource Usage**: Monitor system resources (CPU, memory, disk usage) to ensure your API has enough resources to handle incoming traffic.

Tools for Monitoring Flask APIs:

1. **Prometheus and Grafana**:
    - **Prometheus** is an open-source monitoring and alerting toolkit. It collects metrics from your application, stores them, and enables you to query the data.
    - **Grafana** can be used to visualize the metrics collected by Prometheus, providing dashboards to help you understand the health of your API.

Example of adding Prometheus to Flask:

bash

Copy

```
pip install prometheus-flask-exporter
```

Then, in your Flask app:

python

Copy

```
from prometheus_flask_exporter import PrometheusMetrics

metrics = PrometheusMetrics(app)
```

2. Prometheus will now collect metrics from your Flask API, which you can visualize using Grafana.
3. **Sentry**:
   - **Sentry** is a service for real-time error tracking. It helps you monitor and fix crashes in real-time.
   - You can integrate Sentry with Flask to automatically report errors that occur in production.

Example of adding Sentry to Flask:

bash

Copy

```
pip install sentry-sdk
```

Then, configure it in your app:

python

Copy

```
import sentry_sdk

from sentry_sdk.integrations.flask import FlaskIntegration
```

```
sentry_sdk.init(
    dsn="https://<your-sentry-dsn>",
    integrations=[FlaskIntegration()],
)
```

4. **New Relic**:
    - **New Relic** is a performance monitoring tool that provides detailed insights into how your Flask application is performing in production, including response times, throughput, and error rates.
    - You can integrate New Relic into your Flask app by installing the New Relic agent and configuring it.

Example:

bash

Copy

```
pip install newrelic
```

Add New Relic configuration to your app:

bash

Copy

```
NEW_RELIC_CONFIG_FILE=newrelic.ini newrelic-admin run-program python app.py
```

5.

10.6. Managing API Versions and Migrations in Production

As your Flask API evolves, you may need to manage **API versions** and **database migrations** to ensure backward compatibility and smooth updates. Here's how to handle both in a production environment.

Managing API Versions:

API versioning allows you to make changes to your API while ensuring that existing users can continue to use older versions of the API without breaking their functionality.

1. **URI Versioning**: One of the most common approaches is to include the version number in the URL path.
   Example:
   - /api/v1/resource
   - /api/v2/resource
2. **Header Versioning**: Alternatively, you can version your API by adding a custom header.
   Example:
   - Accept: application/vnd.myapi.v1+json
   - Accept: application/vnd.myapi.v2+json
3. **Semantic Versioning**: Use semantic versioning (e.g., 1.0.0, 1.1.0) to indicate changes and new features in your API. This can be helpful for clients to understand when backward-incompatible changes have been made.

Managing Database Migrations:

As your API grows and evolves, your database schema may change as well. To manage these changes in production, you'll need a strategy for **database migrations**.

Flask-Migrate is a popular extension that integrates with **Alembic** to handle migrations for Flask apps using SQLAlchemy.

Install Flask-Migrate:

bash

Copy

```
pip install flask-migrate
```

1. **Set Up Flask-Migrate**:

   Initialize Flask-Migrate and configure it in your app:

   python

   Copy

```
from flask_migrate import Migrate

from flask_sqlalchemy import SQLAlchemy



app = Flask(__name__)

app.config['SQLALCHEMY_DATABASE_URI'] = 'your-database-uri'

db = SQLAlchemy(app)

migrate = Migrate(app, db)
```

2. **Run Migrations**:

   Initialize the migration repository:

   bash

   Copy

```
flask db init
```

After making changes to your models, generate a migration:

bash

Copy

```
flask db migrate -m "Description of changes"
```

Finally, apply the migration to the production database:

bash

Copy

```
flask db upgrade
```

3. **Handling Downtime**:
   - During critical schema changes, consider using **zero-downtime deployments** where you first apply the migration in a way that maintains compatibility with both old and new API versions.

In this chapter, we explored key strategies for deploying Flask APIs to production. We discussed setting up **Continuous Integration and Continuous Deployment (CI/CD)** pipelines using **GitHub Actions** to automate testing and deployment. We also covered how to monitor your Flask API in production using tools like **Prometheus**, **Sentry**, and **New Relic**. Finally, we learned about **managing API versions** and **database migrations** to ensure that your API remains flexible and scalable as it evolves. With these practices, you can ensure that your Flask API is production-ready, reliable, and easy to maintain.

Chapter 11: Advanced Flask Features

11.1. Advanced Routing: Dynamic Routing and URL Parameters

In Flask, routing is one of the fundamental concepts, and it allows you to map URL patterns to Python functions. While basic routes are simple, Flask also provides powerful features for dynamic routing, allowing you to create more flexible and dynamic endpoints.

Dynamic Routing

Dynamic routes allow you to capture parts of the URL and use them in your functions. This is useful for building RESTful APIs where the route structure may vary depending on the resource being accessed. You can define dynamic routes by using URL parameters.

Defining Dynamic Routes

Dynamic parts of a route are enclosed in angle brackets <>. These dynamic segments are captured and passed as arguments to the view function. Flask automatically converts the value into a Python type based on the route definition.

For example:

python
Copy
```
@app.route('/user/<username>')
def show_user_profile(username):
    return f"User: {username}"
```

In this example:

- The route /user/<username> defines a dynamic segment <username>, which can match any string.
- The username parameter is passed to the show_user_profile function, where it is used to display the user's profile.

Dynamic Route Types

1. **String Parameters**:
   - By default, Flask treats dynamic segments as strings.

Example:

python

Copy

```
@app.route('/post/<slug>')
def show_post(slug):
    return f"Post: {slug}"
```

2. **Integer Parameters**:
   - If you want to enforce that a dynamic parameter is an integer, you can use the <int:parameter> syntax.

Example:

python

Copy

```
@app.route('/post/<int:post_id>')
def show_post(post_id):
    return f"Post ID: {post_id}"
```

3.

4. **Float Parameters**:
    - Similarly, you can use <float:parameter> to capture floating-point numbers.

Example:

python

Copy

```
@app.route('/product/<float:price>')
def show_product(price):
    return f"Product Price: ${price}"
```

5. **Path Parameters**:
    - You can capture entire paths using the <path:parameter> syntax. This captures everything in the URL, including slashes.

Example:

python

Copy

```
@app.route('/files/<path:filename>')
def download_file(filename):
    return f"Downloading: {filename}"
```

6. **Optional Parameters**

You can also define optional parameters in routes by setting default values for them.

Example:

python

Copy

```
@app.route('/post/<int:post_id>/<string:category>')
@app.route('/post/<int:post_id>')
def show_post(post_id, category='general'):
```

```
    return f"Post ID: {post_id}, Category: {category}"
```

In this example, the category parameter is optional. If not provided, it defaults to 'general'.

11.2. Flask Middleware: Customizing Requests and Responses

Flask middleware allows you to run custom logic before or after a request is processed. Middleware can modify incoming requests, handle errors, or modify outgoing responses. Middleware in Flask is implemented using **before request** and **after request** handlers.

Before Request Handlers

A before request handler is a function that runs before any view function is called. This is useful for tasks like authentication checks, logging, or setting up global variables.

To define a before request function, use the @app.before_request decorator:

python
Copy
```
@app.before_request
def before_request():
    print("This function runs before every request")
```

After Request Handlers

After request handlers allow you to modify the response before it is sent to the client. You can use this to add headers, log responses, or handle errors.

To define an after request function, use the @app.after_request decorator:

python

Copy

```
@app.after_request
def after_request(response):
    print("This function runs after each request")
    response.headers['X-Custom-Header'] = 'Value'
    return response
```

Error Handling Middleware

Flask allows you to define custom error handlers using the @app.errorhandler decorator. This is useful for catching and handling exceptions in a consistent way across your application.

Example of handling 404 errors:

python

Copy

```
@app.errorhandler(404)
def page_not_found(e):
    return "Page not found", 404
```

Global Request and Response Modifications

Flask middleware can also be used to modify requests and responses globally. You can customize the request data (e.g., parsing JSON bodies) or add custom headers to responses.

Example of modifying incoming JSON data:

python

Copy

```
@app.before_request
def modify_request_data():
    if request.is_json:
        data = request.get_json()
        # Modify data as needed
        request._cached_json = data
```

Using Flask Middleware for Authentication

One common use case for middleware in Flask is authentication. You can use before request handlers to check for authentication tokens or session cookies before accessing certain routes.

Example of a middleware function that checks for a user token:

python

Copy

```
from flask import request, abort

@app.before_request
def check_authentication():
    token = request.headers.get('Authorization')
    if not token or token != 'secret-token':
        abort(401, description="Unauthorized access")
```

11.3. Using Flask-Login for User Management

Flask-Login is an extension that provides session management and user authentication for Flask applications. It makes it easier to manage user logins, logout functionality, and user session tracking.

Installing Flask-Login

First, install **Flask-Login**:

bash

Copy

```
pip install flask-login
```

Setting Up Flask-Login

To use Flask-Login, you need to create a user model, initialize the LoginManager, and configure user session management.

Create a User Model:

Flask-Login works by using a user object that has certain properties (like is_authenticated, is_active, get_id()). For simplicity, let's assume you're using a SQLAlchemy model for users.

Example:

python

Copy

```
from flask_sqlalchemy import SQLAlchemy

db = SQLAlchemy()

class User(db.Model):
```

```
    id = db.Column(db.Integer, primary_key=True)
    username = db.Column(db.String(80), unique=True, nullable=False)
    password = db.Column(db.String(120), nullable=False)

    def get_id(self):
        return str(self.id)

    def is_authenticated(self):
        return True

    def is_active(self):
        return True

    def is_anonymous(self):
        return False
```

1. **Initialize Flask-Login**:

   Now, you can initialize **Flask-Login** in your Flask app:

   python

   Copy

```
from flask_login import LoginManager

login_manager = LoginManager()
login_manager.init_app(app)

@login_manager.user_loader
def load_user(user_id):
    return User.query.get(int(user_id))
```

2. The @login_manager.user_loader function is called to load the user from the database based on the user's ID stored in the session.

User Login and Logout:

You can create views to log users in and out using **Flask-Login**'s login_user and logout_user functions.

Example of logging a user in:

python

Copy

```
from flask_login import login_user


@app.route('/login', methods=['POST'])
def login():
    username = request.form['username']
    password = request.form['password']
    user = User.query.filter_by(username=username).first()

    if user and user.password == password:
        login_user(user)
        return "Logged in successfully!"
    else:
        return "Invalid credentials", 401
```

Example of logging a user out:

python

Copy

```
from flask_login import logout_user


@app.route('/logout')
def logout():
    logout_user()
```

```
    return "Logged out successfully!"
```

3. **Protecting Routes with login_required**:

   To require that a user is logged in to access a route, use the @login_required decorator:

   python

   Copy

```
from flask_login import login_required


@app.route('/dashboard')
@login_required
def dashboard():
    return "Welcome to your dashboard!"
```

4. This ensures that users who are not authenticated will be redirected to the login page.
5. **Session Management**:

   Flask-Login automatically manages user sessions by storing the user's ID in a secure cookie. This allows users to stay logged in across multiple requests. You can also set session timeout and handling using Flask-Login's settings.

We explored some **advanced features** of Flask that enhance the flexibility and scalability of your web applications. We covered **dynamic routing**, enabling Flask to handle variable URL patterns and parameters. We also looked at **Flask middleware**, allowing for custom logic before and after requests, such as user authentication and error handling. Finally, we introduced **Flask-Login**, a powerful extension for managing user authentication, which simplifies session management and protecting routes.

By mastering these advanced features, you can build more sophisticated and secure APIs with Flask that are ready to handle real-world use cases, including dynamic data, authentication, and customizable behavior.

11.4. Flask-Admin for Admin Interface

Flask-Admin is an extension that provides a simple interface for managing your Flask application's data. It automatically generates an admin panel based on your models, allowing you to perform CRUD operations (Create, Read, Update, Delete) on your application's data without writing any additional code. This is particularly useful for quickly building back-end systems and administrative dashboards.

Setting Up Flask-Admin

Installation:

First, install Flask-Admin:

bash

Copy

```
pip install flask-admin
```

1. **Basic Configuration**:

   After installation, you can integrate Flask-Admin into your Flask application. You need to create an admin interface and bind it to your database models.

   Example:

   python

   Copy

```
from flask import Flask

from flask_sqlalchemy import SQLAlchemy
from flask_admin import Admin
from flask_admin.contrib.sqla import ModelView
```

```
app = Flask(__name__)
app.config['SQLALCHEMY_DATABASE_URI'] = 'sqlite:///mydatabase.db'
db = SQLAlchemy(app)

# Define a model
class User(db.Model):
    id = db.Column(db.Integer, primary_key=True)
    username = db.Column(db.String(80), unique=True, nullable=False)
    email = db.Column(db.String(120), unique=True, nullable=False)

# Initialize Flask-Admin
admin = Admin(app, name='Admin Interface', template_mode='bootstrap3')

# Add a view to Flask-Admin for the User model
admin.add_view(ModelView(User, db.session))

if __name__ == '__main__':
    app.run(debug=True)
```

In this example:

- The User model is defined with id, username, and email fields.
- We initialize the **Flask-Admin** interface and use the ModelView class to create an admin view for the User model.
- The admin panel is automatically populated with forms and data management interfaces based on the User model's fields.

3. **Running the Admin Interface**:
   When you run the Flask app, Flask-Admin automatically generates an admin interface that can be accessed at /admin. The default Flask-Admin interface provides a simple but powerful UI for managing database records.

Customizing Flask-Admin

Flask-Admin is highly customizable. You can:

- Add custom views for more complex models.
- Set access controls for different user roles (e.g., allow certain users to view data but not edit).
- Customize the appearance and behavior of the forms.

For example, to customize the model view to allow only the admin to edit user information, you can add custom permissions:

python

Copy

```
class MyModelView(ModelView):
    def is_accessible(self):
        return current_user.is_authenticated and current_user.is_admin  # Check if the user is an admin

admin.add_view(MyModelView(User, db.session))
```

With **Flask-Admin**, you can rapidly create a fully functional admin interface for your Flask app, allowing you to focus on application logic rather than administrative tools.

11.5. Integrating Flask with Frontend Frameworks (Vue.js, React)

Flask is primarily a back-end framework, but it works seamlessly with modern **frontend frameworks** like **Vue.js** and **React**. These frontend frameworks allow you to build dynamic, interactive web applications, while Flask can handle the back-end logic and API requests.

Using Flask with Vue.js

1. **Setting Up Flask and Vue.js**:
    - The most common way to integrate Flask with Vue.js is by using Flask as an API backend and Vue.js as the frontend.
    - You can build a RESTful API in Flask and make API requests from Vue.js.

Flask Setup (API endpoints):

python

Copy

```python
@app.route('/api/users')
def get_users():
    users = User.query.all()
    return jsonify([user.to_dict() for user in users])


@app.route('/api/user/<int:id>')
def get_user(id):
    user = User.query.get(id)
    if user:
        return jsonify(user.to_dict())
    return jsonify({"error": "User not found"}), 404
```

Vue.js Setup (Fetching data from the API):

javascript

Copy

```javascript
new Vue({
  el: '#app',
```

```
 data: {
  users: []
 },
 mounted() {
  fetch('http://localhost:5000/api/users')
   .then(response => response.json())
   .then(data => {
    this.users = data;
   });
 }
});
```

2. In this setup:
   - Flask serves as the backend that provides the API endpoints.
   - Vue.js makes HTTP requests (using fetch) to retrieve data from Flask and display it in the frontend.
3. **Deployment**:
   - To deploy, you can either serve the Vue.js application from a Flask route by using Flask to serve the static files, or you can use a dedicated web server (e.g., **NGINX**) to serve the Vue.js app and proxy requests to Flask.
4. For example, after building your Vue.js app, you can place the compiled files (e.g., from npm run build) into the Flask static folder and serve them.

Using Flask with React

The integration between Flask and **React** follows a similar approach to Flask with Vue.js. You build Flask APIs for your back-end logic and serve them to the React frontend.

Setting Up Flask (API Backend):
Flask will handle API routes, for example:

python

Copy

```python
@app.route('/api/todos')
def get_todos():
    todos = Todo.query.all()
    return jsonify([todo.to_dict() for todo in todos])
```

1. **React Setup (Frontend)**:

   In your React app, use **Axios** (or **fetch**) to make requests to the Flask API:

   javascript

   Copy

```javascript
import React, { useState, useEffect } from 'react';

import axios from 'axios';

const App = () => {
  const [todos, setTodos] = useState([]);

  useEffect(() => {
    axios.get('http://localhost:5000/api/todos')
      .then(response => {
        setTodos(response.data);
      });
  }, []);

  return (
    <div>
      <h1>Todo List</h1>
      <ul>
        {todos.map(todo => (
```

```
        <li key={todo.id}>{todo.text}</li>
      ))}
    </ul>
  </div>
 );
};

export default App;
```

2. **Deployment**:
   Like with Vue.js, you can deploy React as a static front-end served by Flask or via a dedicated web server. If you're serving it through Flask, make sure to place the compiled React files (from `npm run build`) into Flask's static directory and use Flask routes to serve them.

11.6. Building Real-Time Web Apps with Flask and WebSockets

WebSockets provide a way for the server to send real-time updates to the client. This is ideal for applications that need to display live data, such as chat apps, live notifications, or dashboards. Flask can handle WebSockets with the help of **Flask-SocketIO**, an extension that adds WebSocket support to Flask applications.

Installing Flask-SocketIO

First, install Flask-SocketIO:

bash

Copy

```
pip install flask-socketio
```

Setting Up WebSockets with Flask

Basic Flask-SocketIO Example:

Here's how you can set up a basic WebSocket communication in Flask using **Flask-SocketIO**.

python

Copy

```
from flask import Flask, render_template
from flask_socketio import SocketIO, send

app = Flask(__name__)
socketio = SocketIO(app)

@app.route('/')
def index():
    return render_template('index.html')

@socketio.on('message')
def handle_message(msg):
    print(f"Message received: {msg}")
    send(msg, broadcast=True)

if __name__ == '__main__':
    socketio.run(app)
```

1. **Client-Side WebSocket Example (HTML/JavaScript)**:

   On the client side, you can use JavaScript to interact with the WebSocket.

   html

   Copy

   ```
   <!DOCTYPE html>
   ```

```html
<html lang="en">
<head>
   <meta charset="UTF-8">
   <title>WebSocket Example</title>
   <script src="https://cdn.socket.io/4.0.1/socket.io.min.js"></script>
</head>
<body>
   <h1>WebSocket Chat</h1>
   <input id="messageInput" type="text" placeholder="Type a message">
   <button onclick="sendMessage()">Send</button>
   <ul id="messages"></ul>

   <script>
      const socket = io.connect('http://localhost:5000');
      socket.on('message', function(data) {
         const messages = document.getElementById('messages');
         const newMessage = document.createElement('li');
         newMessage.textContent = data;
         messages.appendChild(newMessage);
      });

      function sendMessage() {
         const message = document.getElementById('messageInput').value;
         socket.send(message);
      }
   </script>
</body>
</html>
```

2. In this setup:

- The server listens for message events sent by the client and broadcasts them to all connected clients.
- The client sends a message to the server using socket.send(), and the server broadcasts the message back to all clients.

Real-Time Features with Flask and WebSockets

WebSockets can be used to implement various real-time features such as:

- **Live Chat**: Allow users to chat in real-time.
- **Notifications**: Push notifications to the client whenever new events occur.
- **Live Data Updates**: Continuously stream data (such as stock prices or weather information) to the client.

Scaling WebSockets

When using WebSockets in production, Flask-SocketIO supports multiple backends for scaling, including **Redis** for message passing between multiple instances of the Flask app. This ensures that messages can be broadcasted across multiple workers in a distributed environment.

In this chapter, we covered some of Flask's **advanced features** to help you build more dynamic and feature-rich web applications. We explored **Flask-Admin**, a tool for quickly creating an admin interface, and discussed how to integrate **Flask with frontend frameworks** like Vue.js and React for building modern single-page applications. Additionally, we dove into building **real-time web apps** using **Flask-SocketIO** and WebSockets, enabling features like live notifications and chat. By mastering these advanced features, you can take your Flask applications to the next level, making them more interactive, user-friendly, and capable of handling complex real-time use cases.

Chapter 12: Case Studies and Real-World Applications

12.1. Building a Social Media API with Flask

Social media platforms typically consist of user management, content creation, comments, likes, and friend requests. Building a social media API involves creating endpoints for user registration, posting content, commenting, and interacting with other users' content. Flask makes it easy to build a RESTful API for such use cases, providing flexibility, simplicity, and extensibility.

Key Features of a Social Media API:

- **User Authentication**: Allow users to sign up, log in, and manage their profiles.
- **Post Creation**: Users can create, edit, and delete posts.
- **Like and Comment System**: Enable users to interact with posts.
- **Friendship System**: Allow users to send and accept friend requests.

Step 1: Setting Up the User Model

First, you'll need a user model for authentication. Here's an example using Flask with SQLAlchemy:

python

Copy

```
from flask import Flask, request, jsonify
from flask_sqlalchemy import SQLAlchemy
from flask_bcrypt import Bcrypt
from flask_login import LoginManager, UserMixin, login_user
```

```
app = Flask(__name__)
app.config['SQLALCHEMY_DATABASE_URI'] = 'sqlite:///social_media.db'
app.config['SECRET_KEY'] = 'secretkey'
db = SQLAlchemy(app)
bcrypt = Bcrypt(app)
login_manager = LoginManager(app)
login_manager.login_view = 'login'

class User(UserMixin, db.Model):
    id = db.Column(db.Integer, primary_key=True)
    username = db.Column(db.String(150), unique=True, nullable=False)
    password = db.Column(db.String(150), nullable=False)
    posts = db.relationship('Post', backref='author', lazy=True)

class Post(db.Model):
    id = db.Column(db.Integer, primary_key=True)
    content = db.Column(db.String(500), nullable=False)
    user_id = db.Column(db.Integer, db.ForeignKey('user.id'), nullable=False)

@login_manager.user_loader
def load_user(user_id):
    return User.query.get(int(user_id))

@app.route('/register', methods=['POST'])
def register():
    data = request.get_json()
    hashed_password = bcrypt.generate_password_hash(data['password']).decode('utf-8')
    user = User(username=data['username'], password=hashed_password)
```

```
    db.session.add(user)
    db.session.commit()
    return jsonify({'message': 'User created successfully'}), 201
```

In this example:

- The **User** model holds user information such as username and password.
- The **Post** model contains the content for posts, and each post is linked to a user via a foreign key.

Step 2: Implementing Post Creation

Users should be able to create, edit, and delete posts. Here's how you might create a new post:

python

Copy

```
@app.route('/post', methods=['POST'])
@login_required
def create_post():
    data = request.get_json()
    post = Post(content=data['content'], user_id=current_user.id)
    db.session.add(post)
    db.session.commit()
    return jsonify({'message': 'Post created successfully'}), 201
```

In this endpoint:

- **@login_required** ensures that only authenticated users can create posts.
- The current_user.id is used to associate the post with the logged-in user.

Step 3: User Interaction (Likes and Comments)

For user interaction, you can create endpoints for commenting on and liking posts. Each of these actions can be represented by a new model, like Comment and Like, with foreign keys linking them to the User and Post models.

Step 4: Building the Friend System

The friend system can be built by creating a **Friendship** model that stores user relationships:

python

Copy

```
class Friendship(db.Model):
    id = db.Column(db.Integer, primary_key=True)
    user_id = db.Column(db.Integer, db.ForeignKey('user.id'), nullable=False)
    friend_id = db.Column(db.Integer, db.ForeignKey('user.id'), nullable=False)
    status = db.Column(db.String(50), nullable=False)  # Pending, Accepted, etc.
```

You can then create endpoints for sending friend requests, accepting requests, and viewing friends.

12.2. Payment Gateway Integration Using Flask

Integrating a payment gateway is a critical part of building an e-commerce application or any platform requiring financial transactions. Payment gateways like **Stripe** or **PayPal** provide APIs that allow you to securely handle credit card transactions, process payments, and manage subscriptions.

Step 1: Setting Up Stripe

Install Stripe Python SDK:

First, you need to install the Stripe Python SDK:

bash

Copy

```
pip install stripe
```

1. **API Keys**:

   You'll need to sign up for a Stripe account and obtain your **API keys** (public and secret) from the Stripe dashboard.

2. **Setting Up Flask for Stripe**:

   Here's a basic Flask route for creating a payment intent with Stripe:

python

Copy

```
import stripe
from flask import Flask, jsonify, request

app = Flask(__name__)
stripe.api_key = "your_stripe_secret_key"

@app.route('/create-payment-intent', methods=['POST'])
def create_payment():
    data = request.get_json()
    amount = data['amount']  # Amount in cents

    try:
        payment_intent = stripe.PaymentIntent.create(
            amount=amount,
            currency='usd',
            payment_method=data['payment_method'],
            confirmation_method='manual',
```

```
        confirm=True
    )
    return jsonify({'client_secret': payment_intent.client_secret}), 200
  except stripe.error.CardError as e:
    return jsonify({'error': str(e)}), 400
```

In this example:

- A payment intent is created with the specified amount and payment method.
- Stripe's error handling is used to catch issues like declined cards.

Step 2: Handling Payment Confirmation on the Frontend

Once the payment intent is created, you need to confirm the payment on the frontend. Using Stripe's **Stripe.js** library, you can handle the confirmation of the payment in the client's browser.

html

Copy

```html
<script src="https://js.stripe.com/v3/"></script>
<script>
  const stripe = Stripe('your_stripe_publishable_key');
  const paymentIntentClientSecret = "client_secret_from_backend";

  stripe.confirmCardPayment(paymentIntentClientSecret, {
    payment_method: {
      card: cardElement,
      billing_details: { name: 'Customer Name' }
    }
  }).then(function(result) {
```

```
    if (result.error) {
      console.log('Payment failed: ' + result.error.message);
    } else {
      console.log('Payment succeeded!');
    }
  });
</script>
```

Step 3: Storing Payment Data

To store payment data securely, ensure that you do not store sensitive information like credit card numbers. Instead, store only the relevant transaction details (e.g., `payment_intent_id`, `amount`, etc.) in your database.

12.3. Building an E-commerce API: Product Listings, Orders, and Payments

An e-commerce API typically involves product management, order processing, and payment handling. Flask is ideal for building these APIs due to its simplicity and flexibility.

Step 1: Product Listings

You can start by creating a **Product** model to store product information like the name, price, description, and image.

python

Copy

```
class Product(db.Model):
```

```
    id = db.Column(db.Integer, primary_key=True)
    name = db.Column(db.String(100), nullable=False)
    description = db.Column(db.String(500), nullable=True)
    price = db.Column(db.Float, nullable=False)
    image_url = db.Column(db.String(200), nullable=True)
```

You can then create an endpoint to retrieve product listings:

python

Copy

```
@app.route('/api/products', methods=['GET'])
def get_products():
    products = Product.query.all()
    return jsonify([product.to_dict() for product in products])
```

This API endpoint retrieves all products from the database and returns them in JSON format.

Step 2: Order Management

Orders typically involve information about the user, the products they are purchasing, and the payment status. You can create an **Order** model like this:

python

Copy

```
class Order(db.Model):
    id = db.Column(db.Integer, primary_key=True)
    user_id = db.Column(db.Integer, db.ForeignKey('user.id'), nullable=False)
    product_id = db.Column(db.Integer, db.ForeignKey('product.id'), nullable=False)
    quantity = db.Column(db.Integer, nullable=False)
```

```
    total_price = db.Column(db.Float, nullable=False)
    payment_status = db.Column(db.String(50), default='Pending')
```

Create an endpoint to place an order:

python

Copy

```
@app.route('/api/orders', methods=['POST'])
def place_order():
    data = request.get_json()
    product = Product.query.get(data['product_id'])
    if product:
        total_price = product.price * data['quantity']
        order = Order(user_id=data['user_id'], product_id=product.id,
quantity=data['quantity'], total_price=total_price)
        db.session.add(order)
        db.session.commit()
        return jsonify({'message': 'Order placed successfully', 'order_id': order.id}), 201
    return jsonify({'error': 'Product not found'}), 404
```

Step 3: Payment Integration

As discussed in **Section 12.2**, you can integrate **Stripe** or any other payment gateway to process payments for the orders. After processing the payment, update the order's payment status:

python

Copy

```
@app.route('/api/payment', methods=['POST'])
```

```
def process_payment():
    order_id = request.json['order_id']
    order = Order.query.get(order_id)

    if order:
        # Process payment via Stripe API (or another payment provider)
        # After successful payment, update the order's status
        order.payment_status = 'Paid'
        db.session.commit()
        return jsonify({'message': 'Payment successful', 'order_id': order.id}), 200
    return jsonify({'error': 'Order not found'}), 404
```

Step 4: Managing Cart and Checkout

You can also add a shopping cart functionality by creating a **Cart** model to store items that a user wants to purchase before checking out.

Example:

python

Copy

```
class Cart(db.Model):
    id = db.Column(db.Integer, primary_key=True)
    user_id = db.Column(db.Integer, db.ForeignKey('user.id'), nullable=False)
    product_id = db.Column(db.Integer, db.ForeignKey('product.id'), nullable=False)
    quantity = db.Column(db.Integer, nullable=False)
```

You can create endpoints to add, remove, or update items in the cart and proceed to checkout when the user is ready to purchase.

We explored three real-world case studies for building APIs with Flask:

1. **Social Media API**: We created basic endpoints for user management, post creation, and a simple friend system.
2. **Payment Gateway Integration**: We integrated a payment gateway (Stripe) for processing transactions securely in Flask.
3. **E-commerce API**: We built a simple e-commerce API with product listings, order processing, and payment handling.

These case studies demonstrate how Flask can be used to build powerful and scalable web applications for real-world business needs, from social media platforms to e-commerce solutions. By following these examples, you can create robust APIs that handle common tasks like user authentication, product management, and payment integration with ease.

12.4. Building a Blogging API with User Authentication and Posts

A blogging platform typically includes features such as user authentication, creating and managing blog posts, editing or deleting posts, and allowing users to comment on posts. Flask's flexibility makes it an excellent choice for building this kind of application. We can start by setting up user authentication and then move on to creating, updating, and deleting blog posts.

Step 1: User Authentication

We'll use **Flask-Login** for handling user authentication and **Flask-Bcrypt** for password hashing.

Install the necessary extensions:

bash

Copy

```
pip install flask-login flask-bcrypt flask_sqlalchemy
```

1. **Setting up the User model**:
   Define the User model with the necessary fields (e.g., username, password).

   python

   Copy

```
from flask import Flask, render_template, request, jsonify

from flask_sqlalchemy import SQLAlchemy

from flask_login import LoginManager, UserMixin, login_user, login_required,
logout_user



app = Flask(__name__)

app.config['SQLALCHEMY_DATABASE_URI'] = 'sqlite:///blog.db'

app.config['SECRET_KEY'] = 'secretkey'

db = SQLAlchemy(app)

login_manager = LoginManager(app)

login_manager.login_view = 'login'



class User(UserMixin, db.Model):

    id = db.Column(db.Integer, primary_key=True)
```

```
    username = db.Column(db.String(150), unique=True, nullable=False)

    password = db.Column(db.String(150), nullable=False)


@login_manager.user_loader

def load_user(user_id):

    return User.query.get(int(user_id))
```

2. **User Registration and Login**:
   Create routes for user registration and login, and ensure that passwords are hashed before saving them in the database.
   python
   Copy

```
from flask_bcrypt import Bcrypt


bcrypt = Bcrypt(app)


@app.route('/register', methods=['POST'])

def register():

    data = request.get_json()

    hashed_password = bcrypt.generate_password_hash(data['password']).decode('utf-8')

    user = User(username=data['username'], password=hashed_password)
```

```
    db.session.add(user)

    db.session.commit()

    return jsonify({'message': 'User registered successfully'}), 201


@app.route('/login', methods=['POST'])

def login():

    data = request.get_json()

    user = User.query.filter_by(username=data['username']).first()

    if user and bcrypt.check_password_hash(user.password, data['password']):

        login_user(user)

        return jsonify({'message': 'Login successful'}), 200

    return jsonify({'message': 'Invalid credentials'}), 401


@app.route('/logout')

@login_required

def logout():

    logout_user()

    return jsonify({'message': 'Logged out successfully'}), 200
```

3. **Step 2: Blog Post Model**

Now that we have user authentication in place, we can proceed to create the blog post model.

python

Copy

```
class Post(db.Model):

    id = db.Column(db.Integer, primary_key=True)

    title = db.Column(db.String(200), nullable=False)

    content = db.Column(db.Text, nullable=False)

    author_id = db.Column(db.Integer, db.ForeignKey('user.id'), nullable=False)

    author = db.relationship('User', backref='posts', lazy=True)
```

Step 3: Creating, Reading, and Deleting Posts

We will create routes for creating, viewing, and deleting posts. Only authenticated users will be able to create or delete posts.

Creating a Post:

python

Copy

```
@app.route('/post', methods=['POST'])

@login_required
```

```
def create_post():

    data = request.get_json()

    new_post = Post(title=data['title'], content=data['content'], author_id=current_user.id)

    db.session.add(new_post)

    db.session.commit()

    return jsonify({'message': 'Post created successfully'}), 201
```

1. **Reading All Posts**:
   python
   Copy
   @app.route('/posts', methods=['GET'])

```
def get_posts():

    posts = Post.query.all()

    return jsonify([{'title': post.title, 'content': post.content, 'author':
post.author.username} for post in posts])
```

2. **Deleting a Post**:
   python
   Copy
   @app.route('/post/<int:id>', methods=['DELETE'])

```
@login_required

def delete_post(id):

    post = Post.query.get_or_404(id)
```

```
    if post.author_id != current_user.id:
        return jsonify({'message': 'Unauthorized'}), 403
    db.session.delete(post)
    db.session.commit()
    return jsonify({'message': 'Post deleted successfully'}), 200
```

Step 4: Commenting on Posts

To allow users to comment on posts, create a `Comment` model and add endpoints for adding and viewing comments.

python

Copy

```
class Comment(db.Model):
    id = db.Column(db.Integer, primary_key=True)
    content = db.Column(db.Text, nullable=False)
    post_id = db.Column(db.Integer, db.ForeignKey('post.id'), nullable=False)
    author_id = db.Column(db.Integer, db.ForeignKey('user.id'), nullable=False)
    post = db.relationship('Post', backref='comments', lazy=True)
    author = db.relationship('User', backref='comments', lazy=True)


@app.route('/post/<int:id>/comment', methods=['POST'])
```

```
@login_required
def comment_on_post(id):
    data = request.get_json()
    post = Post.query.get_or_404(id)
    comment = Comment(content=data['content'], post_id=post.id,
author_id=current_user.id)
    db.session.add(comment)
    db.session.commit()
    return jsonify({'message': 'Comment added successfully'}), 201
```

12.5. Case Study: Scalable Flask API for a High-Traffic Website

Building a Flask API that can handle high traffic requires special attention to scalability and performance. When designing a scalable Flask API, you need to consider various factors like load balancing, database optimization, and caching.

Key Strategies for Scalability:

1. **Load Balancing**:
   Use load balancers (e.g., **NGINX, HAProxy**) to distribute traffic across multiple instances of your Flask application. This ensures that no single instance is overloaded and that requests are handled efficiently.

2. **Database Optimization**:
    - Use database indexing to speed up query performance.
    - Implement **database sharding** or **replication** to scale your database horizontally.
    - Use **ORM optimizations** in SQLAlchemy (e.g., using joinedload or selectinload to avoid N+1 query problems).

Caching:
Use caching strategies like **Redis** to store frequently accessed data, reducing the load on your database. You can cache API responses, user sessions, or other data that doesn't change frequently.
Example of using Redis to cache API responses:
python
Copy

```
from redis import Redis


redis = Redis(host='localhost', port=6379)


@app.route('/posts', methods=['GET'])

def get_posts():

    cached_posts = redis.get('posts')

    if cached_posts:

        return jsonify(cached_posts)

    posts = Post.query.all()
```

```python
    redis.set('posts', posts)  # Cache posts for future requests

    return jsonify([post.to_dict() for post in posts])
```

3. **Asynchronous Task Handling**:
   For tasks that are time-consuming (e.g., sending emails, processing payments), use **Celery** to offload these tasks to background workers. This allows your API to respond quickly without blocking while the task is being processed.
   Example of using Celery with Flask:
   python
   Copy

```python
from celery import Celery

app.config['CELERY_BROKER_URL'] = 'redis://localhost:6379/0'

celery = Celery(app.name, broker=app.config['CELERY_BROKER_URL'])

@celery.task

def send_email(email):

    # Send email in the background

    pass
```

4. **API Rate Limiting**:
   Implement **rate limiting** to prevent abuse and ensure fair use of the API. You can use Flask extensions like **Flask-Limiter** to set limits on API usage.
   python

Copy

```
from flask_limiter import Limiter

limiter = Limiter(app)

@app.route('/api', methods=['GET'])
@limiter.limit('5 per minute')  # Limit to 5 requests per minute
def api():
    return jsonify({'message': 'This is the API'})
```

12.6. Troubleshooting Common Issues in Real-World Projects

In real-world projects, you'll encounter various issues, from performance bottlenecks to security vulnerabilities. Here are some common issues and their solutions:

1. Slow API Response Times:

- **Cause**: Slow database queries or blocking operations.
- **Solution**: Optimize database queries using indexing or caching. Consider offloading time-consuming tasks to background workers using **Celery**. Also, use **profiling tools** (e.g., **Flask-Profiler**) to identify bottlenecks.

2. Database Connection Errors:

- **Cause**: Too many simultaneous database connections or incorrect configuration.

- **Solution**: Use **connection pooling** and **ORM optimizations** to reduce the number of connections. Consider using **read replicas** for read-heavy operations.

3. API Security Vulnerabilities:

- **Cause**: Lack of input validation, CSRF attacks, or weak authentication.
- **Solution**: Implement input validation and use **Flask-WTF** for form handling. Protect APIs with strong authentication (e.g., **OAuth**, **JWT**). Ensure proper **CORS** settings and use **CSRF tokens**.

4. Handling Large File Uploads:

- **Cause**: Large files can overwhelm your Flask application, leading to timeouts.
- **Solution**: Use a **file storage service** (e.g., **Amazon S3**) and limit the file size uploaded. Offload file uploads to background workers using **Celery** to prevent blocking.

5. Memory Leaks:

- **Cause**: Accumulation of unused objects or excessive memory usage by Flask or database connections.
- **Solution**: Use **profiling tools** to identify memory leaks and optimize memory usage. Implement **garbage collection** and ensure proper cleanup of resources (e.g., database connections).

6. Handling High Traffic:

- **Cause**: Flask's default server isn't built for handling high traffic.
- **Solution**: Use a **WSGI server** like **Gunicorn** or **uWSGI** and configure **load balancing** across multiple Flask instances.

In this chapter, we explored a range of **real-world applications** using Flask. We covered building a **blogging API** with user authentication, creating a **scalable Flask API** for high-traffic websites, and troubleshooting common issues faced in production. By following these case studies and strategies, you can build robust, scalable, and secure Flask applications suitable for various use cases, from blogging platforms to e-commerce websites. Troubleshooting and optimizing your applications for performance and scalability will ensure that they run smoothly in production, even under heavy traffic.

Chapter 13: Conclusion and Next Steps

13.1. Summarizing Key Learnings

Throughout this book, we have covered a comprehensive range of topics to help you become proficient in building powerful Flask APIs. Let's summarize the key takeaways:

1. **Flask Basics**:
   - We started by learning the fundamentals of Flask, from setting up a simple application to understanding the core concepts of routing, HTTP methods, and request handling. You now know how to set up and configure a Flask application and define API routes effectively.
2. **Building RESTful APIs**:
   - You've gained a deep understanding of how to create RESTful APIs with Flask, including working with query parameters, request bodies, and handling various HTTP methods (GET, POST, PUT, DELETE).
   - We also covered how to implement features like user authentication, authorization, and token-based systems using **Flask-Login** and **JWT**.
3. **Database Integration**:
   - We explored how to integrate databases with Flask, including using **SQLAlchemy** for relational databases and performing CRUD operations. You also learned how to manage database migrations using **Flask-Migrate**.
4. **Building Real-World Applications**:
   - Case studies allowed you to apply your Flask skills to real-world applications, such as building social media APIs, e-commerce platforms, blogging systems, and payment gateway integrations.

- You've learned how to structure and scale Flask applications for production environments, ensuring that they can handle high traffic and provide a seamless user experience.

5. **Flask Advanced Features**:
    - We delved into advanced features of Flask, such as **middleware**, **dynamic routing**, and **Flask-Admin**. You also gained insight into integrating Flask with frontend frameworks like **Vue.js** and **React**, as well as building real-time web applications using **Flask-SocketIO**.
6. **Deployment and Scaling**:
    - We covered the process of deploying Flask applications to cloud platforms such as **Heroku** and **AWS EC2**, ensuring that your APIs are scalable and secure. You learned how to use **Docker** for containerization and how to implement CI/CD pipelines for seamless deployment.
7. **Troubleshooting and Performance Optimization**:
    - You've learned how to troubleshoot common issues in Flask projects, including slow response times, database connection errors, and API security vulnerabilities. Additionally, we discussed strategies for optimizing performance and scaling your Flask applications.

13.2. How to Keep Improving Your Flask API Skills

Flask is a versatile and powerful framework, and there's always more to learn and experiment with. Here are some tips on how to continue improving your Flask API development skills:

1. **Build More Projects**:
    - The best way to improve your skills is by building more projects. Start with small projects, like creating an API for a to-do list app, and

gradually scale up to more complex applications like social media platforms or e-commerce sites. The more you build, the more you will learn.

2. **Contribute to Open Source**:
    - Contributing to open-source Flask projects is a great way to practice and improve your skills. Not only will you learn from others' code, but you'll also get experience working in real-world projects with other developers.
3. **Explore Advanced Flask Features**:
    - Flask has a wealth of extensions and features that can enhance your API's functionality. Explore **Flask-SocketIO** for real-time communication, **Flask-RESTful** for building APIs, and **Flask-GraphQL** for creating GraphQL APIs. Also, consider learning how to use **Flask with Docker** and **Kubernetes** for container orchestration.
4. **Learn About Web Security**:
    - Security is crucial when building APIs. Dive deeper into security practices like **OAuth 2.0**, **rate-limiting**, **CORS** (Cross-Origin Resource Sharing), and **SQL injection prevention**. Understanding how to protect your API from attacks will help you build secure, production-ready systems.
5. **Optimize Your Code**:
    - Work on optimizing the performance of your Flask applications by learning about profiling tools, database optimizations, and caching strategies. Flask has several tools for improving speed and scalability, such as **Flask-Caching** and **Flask-Profiler**.
6. **Learn Testing and Debugging**:
    - Writing automated tests is a critical part of building reliable applications. Improve your skills in writing unit tests, integration tests, and end-to-end tests using **pytest** and **Flask-Testing**. Understanding how to debug Flask

applications and use profiling tools will also make you a more efficient developer.

7. **Stay Up-to-Date with Flask**:
    - Flask is actively maintained, and new features and updates are released regularly. Keep an eye on the Flask documentation, release notes, and community forums to stay updated on the latest changes. Also, follow Flask-related blogs, podcasts, and online communities to learn new tips and tricks from experienced developers.

13.3. Additional Resources for Flask Development

To continue your Flask development journey, here are some additional resources you can explore:

1. **Official Flask Documentation**:
    - The official Flask documentation is a fantastic resource for understanding Flask's features and best practices. It covers everything from installation to advanced topics like middleware and testing.
    - Website: https://flask.palletsprojects.com
2. **Flask Mega-Tutorial by Miguel Grinberg**:
    - This comprehensive tutorial covers all aspects of Flask development, from basic setup to building complete web applications. It's widely regarded as one of the best resources for Flask developers.
    - Website: https://blog.miguelgrinberg.com/post/the-flask-mega-tutorial-part-i-hello-world

3. **Flask Extensions**:
    - Flask has a rich ecosystem of extensions that add functionality to your app. Check out the Flask Extensions Index to explore extensions for database integration, form handling, authentication, and more.
    - Website: https://flask.palletsprojects.com/en/2.0.x/extensions/
4. **Flask on GitHub**:
    - The Flask GitHub repository contains the source code for Flask and many community-driven projects. By looking at open-source Flask apps, you can learn how large-scale Flask applications are structured.
    - GitHub: https://github.com/pallets/flask
5. **Flask Tutorials on Real Python**:
    - Real Python offers many high-quality tutorials on Flask. These tutorials cover various Flask topics, such as building APIs, web apps, handling forms, and more.
    - Website: https://realpython.com/tutorials/flask/
6. **Flask Community and Forums**:
    - Join the Flask community to ask questions, share ideas, and learn from other Flask developers. The community can be found on platforms like **Stack Overflow**, **Reddit**, and **Flask's own mailing list**.
    - Stack Overflow: https://stackoverflow.com/questions/tagged/flask
    - Reddit: https://www.reddit.com/r/flask/
7. **Books on Flask**:
    - **"Flask Web Development" by Miguel Grinberg**: This book offers a comprehensive guide to Flask, starting from the basics and moving to advanced topics.
    - **"Mastering Flask" by Jack Stouffer**: This book dives into more complex Flask patterns, including how to structure large applications and scale them.

8. **Courses and Video Tutorials**:
   - Platforms like **Udemy**, **Coursera**, and **Pluralsight** offer excellent Flask courses that provide hands-on experience with real-world projects. Look for courses that focus on building full-stack applications or APIs with Flask.

Flask is a powerful and flexible framework for building web applications and APIs, and with the knowledge gained from this book, you are now equipped to build, deploy, and scale production-ready Flask APIs. Whether you're interested in building a simple blog or a complex e-commerce platform, Flask provides all the tools you need to succeed.

The journey doesn't stop here. Keep building, experimenting, and exploring new Flask features and best practices. Flask's flexibility makes it ideal for all kinds of projects, and with continuous learning, you'll be able to tackle even more ambitious projects with confidence.

13.4. Staying Updated with the Latest Flask and Python Features

The world of web development, including Flask and Python, evolves quickly. New versions of Flask and Python regularly introduce features, improvements, and optimizations that can help you write cleaner code, build more efficient applications, and take advantage of the latest best practices. Staying updated with these changes is essential for keeping your projects modern and efficient.

How to Stay Updated:

1. **Follow the Flask and Python Release Notes**:
   - Flask and Python both have detailed release notes that explain new features, bug fixes, and breaking changes in each version. By keeping

track of these, you can ensure your projects stay compatible with the latest versions of these tools.

   - Flask release notes: https://flask.palletsprojects.com/en/latest/changes/
   - Python release notes: https://docs.python.org/3/whatsnew/

2. **Subscribe to Flask and Python Blogs**:
   - Many developers and official project maintainers publish blogs detailing the latest features and updates. Subscribing to these blogs will keep you informed about significant changes.
   - **Flask Blog**: https://blog.palletsprojects.com/
   - **Python Software Foundation Blog**: https://www.python.org/blogs/
3. **Follow Flask and Python on Social Media**:
   - Twitter, Reddit, and other social media platforms are great for real-time updates. Following the official accounts and hashtags can help you stay in the loop about new features, frameworks, tools, and practices.
   - **Flask Twitter**: @Flask
   - **Python Twitter**: @ThePSF
4. **Participate in Online Communities**:
   - Online forums, discussion boards, and communities like **Stack Overflow**, **Reddit**, and **Discord** have active members who often discuss the latest features, new releases, and the future direction of Flask and Python. These communities are great for learning about new tools, libraries, and trends in Flask development.
   - **Reddit Flask Community**: r/flask
   - **Python Reddit Community**: r/Python
5. **Follow Key Developers and Experts**:
   - Many Flask and Python experts share their insights on the latest features and development trends. By following key figures in the community, you can stay ahead of the curve.
   - **Miguel Grinberg** (creator of the Flask Mega-Tutorial): @miguelgrinberg

- **Armin Ronacher** (Flask creator): @mitsuhiko

6. **Attend Webinars, Meetups, and Conferences**:
    - Participating in community events, such as webinars, conferences, and meetups, allows you to hear about new developments, best practices, and emerging tools from experienced developers and project maintainers.
    - Look for events such as **PyCon**, **FlaskCon**, and **local Python meetups** to stay updated on the latest Flask and Python developments.
7. **Explore New Python Features**:
    - Python frequently introduces new features and syntax improvements. For example, recent Python versions introduced **f-strings** for easier string formatting, **data classes** for simple data structures, and improvements to **async programming**. Familiarizing yourself with these features can help you write more Pythonic code and enhance your projects.
    - Keep an eye on new **Python Enhancement Proposals (PEPs)** to understand upcoming changes. PEPs often detail new features, optimizations, and language changes in Python.
8. **Test New Features with Your Projects**:
    - When a new version of Flask or Python is released, don't be afraid to experiment with it in your projects. While it's important to maintain compatibility for production applications, testing new features in your development environment will help you get a jump start on utilizing them in your projects.

13.5. Community and Collaboration: Contributing to Open Source Flask Projects

Contributing to open-source projects is an excellent way to learn more, collaborate with others, and improve your Flask and Python skills. Open-source projects offer a wealth of experience, allowing you to gain insight into best practices, code quality, and how large-scale applications are built.

Why Contribute to Open Source Flask Projects?

1. **Gain Real-World Experience**:
   - Working on open-source projects exposes you to real-world problems and solutions. You'll learn how to write high-quality, maintainable code, and you'll work with other developers who follow industry best practices.
2. **Build a Strong Portfolio**:
   - Contributing to open-source projects enhances your portfolio and helps establish your credibility as a developer. It shows future employers that you're actively involved in the community and willing to take on complex, collaborative projects.
3. **Learn New Technologies and Practices**:
   - Open-source projects often adopt cutting-edge tools, libraries, and workflows. Contributing to these projects allows you to stay up to date with the latest trends in Flask and Python development.
4. **Develop Collaboration Skills**:
   - Open-source development is collaborative. You'll work with others on bug fixes, feature development, code reviews, and documentation. These interactions will improve your communication, teamwork, and problem-solving abilities.

5. **Help the Community**:
   - By contributing to open-source Flask projects, you'll help others who rely on these tools. It's a way of giving back to the community and improving resources that developers worldwide use.

Where to Find Flask Open Source Projects to Contribute To?

1. **GitHub**:
   - GitHub is the largest platform for open-source projects. Search for Flask-related repositories to find projects that interest you. Many Flask projects have labels like **"good first issue"** or **"help wanted"** for newcomers.
   - Flask's official GitHub repository: https://github.com/pallets/flask
2. **Flask Extensions**:
   - Contributing to Flask extensions is a great way to get involved. There are hundreds of extensions available for Flask, covering everything from database integration to authentication. Explore the Flask extensions list and find projects that align with your interests.
   - Flask extensions list: https://flask.palletsprojects.com/en/latest/extensions/
3. **Flask Projects on GitHub**:
   - Look for projects that use Flask in their backend. These projects may have open issues or requests for contributors. You can start by searching for Flask-based projects on GitHub or use specific search queries like "Flask API" or "Flask app."
4. **Hacktoberfest**:
   - Hacktoberfest is an annual event where developers around the world contribute to open-source projects. Many Flask and Python projects participate in Hacktoberfest, and it's an excellent opportunity for newcomers to start contributing.

- Website: https://hacktoberfest.digitalocean.com/

5. **Python and Flask Communities**:
   - Flask and Python communities are full of open-source projects that need contributions. Participate in forums like **Stack Overflow**, **Reddit**, or **Discord** communities to connect with people who maintain open-source Flask projects.
6. **Contributing to Documentation**:
   - If you're new to open-source contributions, one of the easiest ways to start is by improving documentation. Many Flask projects need better explanations, examples, or updated content. Contributing to documentation is a valuable way to help while learning about the project.

How to Start Contributing:

1. **Start with Issues**:
   - Begin by checking out the open issues in the repository. Look for issues labeled **"good first issue"** or **"help wanted"**, which are specifically aimed at newcomers.
   - If the repository has a **contributing guide**, make sure to read it before submitting a pull request (PR). The contributing guide will outline the project's process for contributions, including coding standards, how to set up the development environment, and testing guidelines.
2. **Fork and Clone the Repository**:
   - To start working on an issue, fork the repository to your own GitHub account. Then, clone the repository to your local machine and create a new branch for your work.
3. **Work on the Issue**:
   - Implement the feature, fix the bug, or improve the documentation as described in the issue. Be sure to test your changes thoroughly.

4. **Submit a Pull Request**:
   - Once your changes are ready, submit a pull request (PR) with a detailed description of what you've done. Be open to feedback from project maintainers and other contributors. They may ask for changes or improvements before merging your PR.
5. **Review Other PRs**:
   - After contributing your own PRs, consider reviewing PRs from other contributors. This helps the community grow, and you will learn a lot by reviewing other people's code.
6. **Stay Consistent**:
   - Try to contribute regularly, even if it's just small fixes or documentation improvements. Consistent contributions will help you become a trusted member of the open-source community.

You now have a clear understanding of how to **stay updated with Flask and Python features** and the benefits of **contributing to open-source Flask projects**. Continuing your Flask journey involves constant learning, experimenting with new features, and engaging with the vibrant Flask community. Whether you're building your own applications, contributing to open-source projects, or simply staying updated with the latest developments, there is always room for growth in the world of Flask development.

Your commitment to improving your skills and collaborating with others will not only advance your career but also help you build a strong presence in the open-source community. So, keep coding, stay curious, and get involved in open-source contributions—there's a whole world of Flask and Python development out there to explore!

Appendices

A.1. Flask Cheat Sheet: Common Commands and Methods

This cheat sheet provides quick references for common Flask commands and methods that are used in building and managing Flask applications.

Flask Application Setup:

Create a Flask App:

python

Copy

```
from flask import Flask
app = Flask(__name__)
```

- **Running the Flask App**:

  bash

  Copy

  ```
  flask run
  ```

- **Set the Flask environment** (for development):

  bash

  Copy

  ```
  export FLASK_ENV=development
  ```

- **Set the Flask App** (for app discovery):

  bash

  Copy

  ```
  export FLASK_APP=your_app.py
  ```

- **Routes:**

Basic Route:

python

Copy

```
@app.route('/')
def home():
    return 'Hello, Flask!'
```

- **Route with Dynamic URL Parameter**:

  python

  Copy

```
@app.route('/user/<username>')

def show_user(username):
    return f"Hello, {username}!"
```

- **HTTP Methods**:

GET (default):

python

Copy

```
@app.route('/get_data', methods=['GET'])
def get_data():
    return 'GET request'
```

  - **POST**:

    python

    Copy

```
@app.route('/submit', methods=['POST'])

def submit():
    data = request.form['data']
```

```
    return 'POST request'
```

- **Request and Response:**

Getting Data from Request:

python

Copy

```
from flask import request
data = request.form['key']  # For form data
json_data = request.json  # For JSON data
```

- **Returning a JSON Response**:

  python

  Copy

  ```
  from flask import jsonify
  ```

```
@app.route('/json')
def json_response():
    return jsonify({"key": "value"})
```

- **Templates:**

Rendering HTML Templates:

python

Copy

```
from flask import render_template
@app.route('/home')
def home():
    return render_template('home.html', name="Flask User")
```

- **Error Handling:**

Custom Error Handler:

python

Copy

```
@app.errorhandler(404)
def page_not_found(e):
    return 'Page not found', 404
```

- **Flask Extensions:**

SQLAlchemy for database integration:

python

Copy

```
from flask_sqlalchemy import SQLAlchemy
db = SQLAlchemy(app)
```

- **Flask-Migrate** for migrations:

  bash

  Copy

```
flask db init

flask db migrate
flask db upgrade
```

A.2. API Security Best Practices Reference

Securing your Flask API is critical for protecting sensitive data and ensuring the integrity of your application. Here are some best practices for securing your Flask APIs:

1. Authentication and Authorization:

- Use **OAuth 2.0**, **JWT (JSON Web Tokens)**, or **API keys** for secure authentication.
- Implement role-based access control (RBAC) to restrict access to certain endpoints based on user roles.

2. Encrypt Sensitive Data:

- Use **HTTPS** (SSL/TLS) to encrypt data in transit between the client and server.
- Hash sensitive information like passwords using **bcrypt** or **argon2**.

3. Rate Limiting:

- Implement **rate limiting** to protect your API from abuse and DoS (Denial of Service) attacks.
- Use tools like **Flask-Limiter** to enforce request limits.

4. Cross-Site Scripting (XSS) Protection:

- Sanitize user inputs to prevent XSS attacks.
- Use **Flask-WTF** and **Jinja2** to automatically escape variables in templates.

5. Cross-Site Request Forgery (CSRF) Protection:

- Enable **CSRF protection** using **Flask-WTF** to prevent malicious forms from submitting data on behalf of users.

6. Input Validation:

- Always validate inputs from users (e.g., using **WTForms** or **Marshmallow**).
- Validate all incoming data to prevent SQL injection, command injection, and other attacks.

7. Secure Headers:

- Set **security headers** such as Content-Security-Policy, Strict-Transport-Security, and X-Content-Type-Options to enhance security.

8. Error Handling:

- Avoid exposing sensitive information in error messages (e.g., database or server details).
- Implement custom error handling that provides generic messages without revealing internal system information.

A.3. Flask Testing Utilities and Tools

Testing is essential for ensuring the reliability and functionality of your Flask application. Below are some tools and utilities for testing Flask APIs:

1. Pytest:

- Pytest is a popular testing framework for Python. To test Flask applications, you can use pytest-flask, an extension for Flask that provides helper functions to test Flask apps.

Example of using **pytest** with Flask:

python
Copy

```
import pytest
from myapp import app

@pytest.fixture
```

```
def client():
    with app.test_client() as client:
        yield client


def test_home(client):
    response = client.get('/')
    assert response.data == b"Hello, Flask!"
```

2. Flask-Testing:

- **Flask-Testing** provides utilities for testing Flask applications, including setup for test databases and convenient assertions.

Example:

python

Copy

```
from flask_testing import TestCase
from myapp import app

class TestHomePage(TestCase):
    def create_app(self):
        app.config['TESTING'] = True
        return app

    def test_home(self):
        response = self.client.get('/')
        self.assert200(response)
```

3. Mocking:

- Mocking helps simulate external services like APIs or databases. Use **unittest.mock** or **pytest-mock** to mock parts of your application during testing.

4. Coverage:

- Use **coverage.py** to measure how much of your code is covered by tests. This ensures that you're testing the core functionality of your app.

To run coverage:

bash

Copy

```
coverage run -m pytest
coverage report
```

A.4. Docker Command Reference for Flask APIs

Docker is a great tool for containerizing Flask applications, ensuring consistency across environments. Below are the most useful Docker commands for Flask API development.

1. Building a Docker Image:

- Build your Flask Docker image using the `docker build` command.

bash

Copy

```
docker build -t flask-api .
```

2. Running a Docker Container:

- Start a Docker container for your Flask app and map ports for external access.

bash

Copy

```
docker run -p 5000:5000 flask-api
```

3. Viewing Logs:

- View the logs of a running container to diagnose issues.

bash

Copy

```
docker logs <container_id>
```

4. Stopping a Container:

- Stop a running container.

bash

Copy

```
docker stop <container_id>
```

5. Removing a Container:

- Remove a stopped container from your system.

bash

Copy

```
docker rm <container_id>
```

6. Running Docker Compose:

- Use Docker Compose to manage multi-container applications.

bash

Copy

```
docker-compose up --build
```

7. Listing Docker Images:

- List all Docker images available on your machine.

bash

Copy

```
docker images
```

A.5. Useful Flask Extensions and Libraries

Flask's ecosystem is rich with extensions that enhance its capabilities. Here are some useful extensions and libraries for building Flask APIs:

1. Flask-SQLAlchemy:

- Integrates SQLAlchemy ORM with Flask for handling database operations.
- Documentation: https://flask-sqlalchemy.palletsprojects.com

2. Flask-Login:

- Adds user session management and authentication to Flask.

- Documentation: https://flask-login.readthedocs.io

3. Flask-WTF:

- Provides integration with WTForms for easy form handling and validation.
- Documentation: https://flask-wtf.readthedocs.io

4. Flask-Migrate:

- Database migrations support using **Alembic** with Flask.
- Documentation: https://flask-migrate.readthedocs.io

5. Flask-RESTful:

- Helps in building REST APIs with Flask.
- Documentation: https://flask-restful.readthedocs.io

6. Flask-SocketIO:

- Enables real-time communication via WebSockets.
- Documentation: https://flask-socketio.readthedocs.io

7. Flask-CORS:

- Provides Cross-Origin Resource Sharing (CORS) support for Flask applications.
- Documentation: https://flask-cors.readthedocs.io

8. Flask-Cache:

- Adds caching support to Flask to improve performance.
- Documentation: https://flask-cache.readthedocs.io

A.6. Recommended Reading and Learning Resources

To deepen your Flask knowledge and further develop your skills, consider exploring the following resources:

1. Books:

- **Flask Web Development** by Miguel Grinberg: A comprehensive guide to mastering Flask, covering everything from basic concepts to advanced features.
- **Mastering Flask Web Development** by Jack Stouffer: An advanced-level book focused on building scalable Flask applications.

2. Online Tutorials and Courses:

- **Real Python**: Offers a series of in-depth Flask tutorials and articles.
  - Website: https://realpython.com
- **Udemy**: Find various courses on Flask API development and advanced Flask features.
- **Flask Mega-Tutorial** by Miguel Grinberg: A great tutorial for beginners to advanced users.

3. Flask Documentation:

- The official Flask documentation is the best place to start learning Flask and its features.
  - Website: https://flask.palletsprojects.com

4. Community and Forums:

- Participate in online communities such as **Stack Overflow**, **Reddit**, or **Flask Google Group** to ask questions and learn from other developers.

This appendix has provided essential references to help you navigate Flask development more effectively. By leveraging these tools, commands, and resources, you can continue to enhance your Flask skills and build scalable, secure, and high-performing APIs. Keep experimenting, building, and learning!

www.ingramcontent.com/pod-product-compliance
Lightning Source LLC
LaVergne TN
LVHW051442050326
832903LV00030BD/3195